Wiring the
Brain for
Reading

Wiring the *Brain* for *Reading*

Brain-Based
Strategies for
Teaching Literacy

Marilee Sprenger

JOSSEY-BASS
A Wiley Imprint
www.josseybass.com

Published by Jossey-Bass
A Wiley Imprint
One Montgomery Street, Suite 1200, San Francisco, CA 94104-4594—www.josseybass.com

Library of Congress Cataloging-in-Publication Data

Sprenger, Marilee, 1949–
  Wiring the brain for reading: brain-based strategies for teaching literacy / Marilee Sprenger.
    pages cm
  Includes bibliographical references and index.
  ISBN 978-0-470-58721-8 (pbk.) ISBN 978-1-118-22054-2 (ebk.) ISBN 978-1-118-23414-3 (ebk.)
ISBN 978-1-118-25891-0 (ebk.)
  1. Reading. 2. Child development. 3. Brain—Growth. I. Title.
LB1573.S8215 2013
372.4—dc23

                                                                                      2012051506

Printed in the United States of America
FIRST EDITION
PB Printing   10 9 8 7 6 5 4 3 2 1

Contents

Acknowledgments

NONE OF MY WORK WOULD BE POSSIBLE without the support of my family. To my husband, Scott, you support my writing, speaking, and traveling. Knowing you are behind me as well as beside me makes everything worthwhile. To my favorite son, Josh, you help me see the big picture and keep me practical. I respect your advice and need your influence in my life. To Marnie, my favorite daughter, thank you for believing in me and keeping me real. You call it as you see it, and I value both your knowledge and opinion. To the second author in the family, my daughter-in-law, Amy: your love of reading and writing have been inspirational for me. I look forward to many best-sellers from you. To my three incredible grandchildren, Jack, Emmie, and Maeve, watching each of you acquire the skills of reading is both educational and delightful. Seeing you excited about books always brings a smile to my face and warmth to my heart.

I thank Kate Bradford, senior editor at Jossey-Bass/Wiley, for her incredible patience and expert assistance; Robin Lloyd, excellent production editor; and Diane Turso, proofreader extraordinaire.

In memory of my mothe
Mollie Brom
the woman who taught n
how to read, to love readin
and to read everything I s

About the Author

MARILEE SPRENGER IS A HIGHLY REGARDED educator, presenter, and author who has taught students from prekindergarten through graduate school. She has been translating neuroscience research for over twenty years and has engaged audiences internationally. The author of eight books and numerous articles, Marilee is a popular keynote speaker who is passionate about brain research–based teaching strategies, which include differentiated instruction and wiring the brain for success.

Marilee is a member of the American Academy of Neurology, the Learning and the Brain Society, and the Cognitive Neuroscience Society. She is an adjunct professor at Aurora University, teaching graduate courses on brain-based teaching, learning and memory, and differentiation. Teachers who have read her work or heard her speak agree that they walk away with user-friendly information that they can apply at all levels.

You can contact Marilee at brainlady@gmail.com or visit her website, brainlady.com.

About the Book

THERE IS NOTHING MORE EXCITING THAN having the privilege of helping people, children and adults, learn to read. The thrill of seeing the smile on their faces and the sparkle in their eyes as they realize they have broken the code is priceless.

Mary Ann Wolfe tells us in *Proust and the Squid* (2007) that learning to read begins the first time a book is read to an infant. This often happens in an environment filled with love for the child and the love of reading. Unfortunately, not all readers have that magical moment that provides security and attachment for the developing brain. There are children who come from homes filled with books and a love of reading. Their parents read aloud to them nightly and have elaborate conversations with them that increase their vocabulary and background knowledge. And then there are students who come to us from homes where literacy is limited. Their parents work long hours and have little time or energy to provide the background that encourages reading. Although there is no guarantee, children who come from homes filled with reading seem to have a better chance at reading success.

In this book, I share some of what I have learned about reading through my own teaching experiences, neuroscience research, and educational research and the experiences of teachers with whom I have had the privilege to work. The science of the brain has revealed exciting and important information that, when added to the educational research, creates standards for best practices in teaching reading.

There are six thousand languages in the world, and babies are born with the ability to master any of them. But the brain changes as children develop, and language acquisition can become more difficult. In chapter 1, discover how children learn their native language and how the brain's approach to new languages changes with age. Developing language is exciting for parents, children, and teachers. Research is continually being done to educate us more about how to encourage better language skills.

Through brain imaging, neuroscientists have discovered what neural connections are necessary for a brain to read easily. Chapter 2 covers the theories and applications of this research. For example, neuronal recycling is necessary for a reading pathway to form, and an understanding of how this and other parts of the brain function helps educators develop best practice and parents how to make a difference in their child's reading progress.

Reading readiness relies on the body as well as the brain. Chapter 3 introduces physical movements that enhance the brain's ability to read. The brain-body connection is powerful. Scientists believe that significant brain development occurs through movement and play.

Chapter 4 reveals how the path to reading begins. Phonemic awareness is the first step toward learning the alphabetic code. Although this skill is emphasized in kindergarten and first grade, it is important for all teachers and parents to understand the significance of making sound and letter connections. Examples of relevant activities are provided in this and other chapters.

After breaking the alphabetic code, the brain needs to be taught how to recognize patterns. Phonics is introduced in chapter 5. The task of learning to read now becomes visual as well as auditory as students learn how to associate sounds with visual representations. Phonics teaches students the most common sound-spelling relationships so that they can decode, or sound out, words.

The next logical step in teaching reading is fluency. Chapter 6 discusses what fluency is and why it matters. The ability to read with expression, speed, and accuracy allows the brain to focus on the content of the reading and enables better comprehension.

Chapter 7 covers teaching vocabulary. The importance of having a large vocabulary is reflected in two important research discoveries: that 85 percent of standardized tests are based on vocabulary and that vocabulary is one way to increase academic background knowledge (Marzano & Pickering, 2005). Learn which vocabulary words from the Common Core State Standards (CCSS) are vital to success, as well as strategies to increase tier 2 words (high-frequency words that occur across a variety of domains), which are considered a large part of the mature reader's vocabulary.

Finally, chapter 8 focuses on reading comprehension. Discover how working memory aids with comprehension and learn many before-, during-, and after-reading strategies to enhance comprehension and memory.

The CCSS heavily emphasize students' ability to read complex text independently and proficiently at every level of development, from kindergarten through grade 12. In order for this to take place, all teachers need the skills to recognize reading difficulties and have strategies to assist struggling readers. Teaching students how to read closely and deeply using a strategy like questioning will help reveal where in the reading process a problem may lie. For instance, if a student cannot summarize what she reads, the teacher or parent can ask who, what, where, why, and how questions to get at the heart of the matter: a memory problem, a vocabulary issue, or an inability to sound out words properly. They can take use information to find a starting point to help train the learner's brain for reading.

CHAPTER 1

Language Development

MAEVE WAS BORN ALREADY RECOGNIZING THE voices of her mother and father. She had been able to hear her mother while in the womb as soon as her ability to hear sound developed by the end of the second trimester of the pregnancy. Soon after, as Maeve's daddy started reading to her and speaking to her in his soothing voice while keeping his mouth close to her mother's belly, she began to respond to the sound of his voice. The clarity of such verbiage to the unborn child has been questioned. But the moment Maeve was born, she responded and turned toward the voices of both Mommy and Daddy.

Maeve's brain at birth will allow her to learn any language and repeat any phonemes (the individual sounds that make up a language) that she hears. If she has been born into a bilingual or multilingual family, she will easily learn the languages that are spoken to her. This ability is short-lived, however. By the time Maeve has been on Earth a year, her brain will have pruned away the neurons (the brain cells that do the learning) that were not used. In other words, her ability to hear some phonemes will be gone or at least partially diminished. She will focus on the sounds that she hears, and by approximately eight months of age, she will begin to attempt to mimic those sounds. Along with the vowels and consonants she will mimic, she may also express other phonemes that are available to her developing brain. Her parents, however, will recognize only the sounds that they know. So when Maeve begins to babble a string of sounds like, "ma, ba, goo, eh, neh, un," what her parents pick up on (especially Mom) is the first sound, "ma." So Mom begins to repeat the sound while she beams at Maeve. "Ma, ma, ma … you said my name: ma, ma, ma." Eventually Maeve gets the idea that this particular sound gets a great response from her mother, and she will begin to repeat the sound to please her mother and get instant feedback. It doesn't matter that within her babbling, she may have shared phonemes from multiple other languages. Since no one will repeat these back to her, she won't strengthen the connections for those sounds. As language is learned, brain cells connect to remember and recreate the sounds that are heard, but connections that are not used often grow weak and unusable.

There are almost seven thousand languages in the world, and babies are born with the ability to master any of them. But the brain changes as children develop, and language acquisition can become more difficult. In order to be able to read, a child must first learn the sounds of the language.

From Neural Sensitivity to Neural Commitment

After an infant is six to nine months of age, only those neurons that have learned the sounds of the language's phonemes spoken to the baby remain. They gain in strength and connections as they are repeated. As this specialization occurs, neurons become committed to those sounds (Bronson & Merryman, 2009).

In 2007, a study by Zimmerman, Dimitri, and Meltzoff stated that DVDs and videos directed to babies are actually harmful to them. The researchers had found that infants who watched these DVDs and videos had smaller vocabularies than babies who did not watch. In fact, the more television a child watched, the fewer vocabulary words he or she knew. The authors of the study gave possible reasons for the vocabulary differences they found:

- Some parents put their children in front of the television for up to twenty hours per week. They thought watching this material would help with brain development, but in fact it meant less time that the babies spent with people talking directly to them.

- Learning speech is partially a process of reading lips. Babies need to see people speaking in order to learn how to move their mouths and lips. Many baby DVDs instead show abstract pictures with voices talking about them.

- It is not possible to segment sounds in speech without seeing people speaking.

- These videos and DVDs lacked the visual and auditory components of speech interaction that are appealing to babies, that is, a face and voice to perform for and respond to.

Videos and DVDs could be made for infants with people speaking directly to the screen, and that might make a little difference. However, this would still leave out the most important component of learning to speak: human interaction.

A recent study published in the *Proceedings of National Academy of Sciences* suggests that babies lip-read as they learn language (Lewkowicz & Hansen-Tift, 2012). The study, from Florida Atlantic University, was conducted using 179 babies aged four, six, ten, and twelve months from English-speaking families. The study stated that the four-month-olds looked at the eyes of the speaker, but as the children got closer to beginning to babble, their gaze shifted from eyes to mouth. By six months of age, the babies spent half of their time looking at the eyes of the speaker and the remaining time at their lips. The eight- and ten-month-old babies spent most of their time watching the mouth of the speaker. As the babies prepared to begin speaking, most at the age of twelve months, their gaze shifted back to eyes. Confirming the need for lip reading was accomplished by having these babies watch a Spanish speaker.

Nature Versus Nurture

Are children born with an innate ability to speak, or is it their experiences and their environment that pave the way for language? Although the brain was once described as a tabula rasa, a blank slate, many researchers believe that the answer lies somewhere in between a blank slate and a preprogrammed mind.

Although children are born with the ability to learn speech, language learning does not occur in a vacuum. Babies don't begin speaking a language that they have never heard. Little Maeve will learn to speak English because her parents and others in her environment speak only English. If Maeve's Russian grandmother lived in the home and spoke only Russian, Maeve would easily pick up that language, too.

Again the eyes shifted to the mouth so babies could see how the sounds were formed.

When Maeve begins to babble, she will make sounds that imitate the phonemes that she has been exposed to and also some sounds from other languages that she has not heard. She will simply be producing whatever sounds she can. Once she becomes more aware of her own language, she will repeat the sounds that she hears.

The Right Way to Babble

It may be hard to believe that babbling has been researched, but the University of Memphis has researchers who have done just that. Analyzing the sounds that babies make beginning at birth (Oller, 2010) has uncovered some interesting milestones in the process of learning language.

Babbling is an element of brain development in both social and emotional areas as well as cognitive development. It represents the learning that is taking place in relationship to language, and it is also an attempt to communicate and interact with the caregiver. A baby who isn't babbling in a typical way may have problems hearing or processing sounds, or perhaps the baby's brain is not being introduced to enough words.

According to pediatrician Perri Klass, babies babble in all of the world's languages. It is a universal sign of neurological development and an indicator of speech readiness. From babbling, infants and toddlers move on to making the sounds of their language and create words appropriate to their environments.

If a baby is not making those combined consonant vowel sounds, there may be a problem. By seven months (remember that development can vary among babies), if the baby is making only vowel sounds, the baby is not getting the practice she needs to begin to form words. Her mouth and tongue are not working the muscles necessary for good speech either (Stoel-Gammon, 2001).

Babbling may be a signal that babies are focused for learning, indicating an opportunity to have the baby's attention as he explores the world and wants to name the objects and people around him.

Encouraging Speech

Parenting experts offer some of the following suggestions for encouraging babies to use their language:

- *Talk a lot.* Between birth and three months, babies begin to acquire language, even though they cannot yet speak, so parents and caregivers are encouraged to talk to babies often.

- *Point out things.* As you talk to the infant, name items and describe what is going on.

- *Help the infant listen.* Point out the sounds around him: "Do you hear the clock?" "Is the dog barking?"

- *Play games.* The rhythm, rhyme, and play of games such as "Peek-a-boo" and "Pat-a-Cake" show the child that language is fun.

Studies have shown that babies whose mothers talk a lot have larger vocabularies than those whose mothers talk very little. It is possible, however, to take talking to the baby too far. Talking at a baby nonstop is not what promotes good language. Asking questions and responding to what the child says are also important.

The most famous study of children and language was carried out by Betty Hart and Todd Risley from the University of Kansas. Although an older study (1995), it is often still considered the gold standard when it comes to determining language development in children. In this groundbreaking work, researchers went into the homes of families of varying socioeconomic status and videotaped the parents as they interacted with their babies, who were between seven and nine months old at the beginning of the study. The taping was done once a month until the children were three years old.

In their book *Meaningful Differences in the Everyday Experiences of Young American Children* (1995), Hart and Risley state, "By age 3 the children in professional families would have heard more than 30 million words, the children in working class families 20 million, and the children in welfare families 10 million" (p. 132). Although the number of words spoken was different, the style of speech and the topics were similar. The more the parents spoke, however, the more likely they were to ask the child questions and the more varied the vocabulary became, so the children received more experience with different language qualities.

In addition to counting the number of words that parents spoke to the children, Hart and Risley also examined the types of reinforcement the children received. Table 1.1 shows the number

Table 1.1 Affirmatives and Prohibitions Given per Hour

	Words Heard per Hour	Affirmatives per Hour	Prohibitions per Hour
Professional family child	2,153	32	5
Working-class family child	1,251	12	7
Welfare family child	616	5	11

of affirmative statements versus prohibitory statements tallied for each socioeconomic group. An example of an affirmation is "Nice job. You are doing a great job!" A prohibition may be something like "Don't do it that way. Can't you do anything right?" The professional parents offered affirmative feedback much more often (every other minute) than the other groups, and the welfare parents gave their children more than twice as many prohibitions as the professional parents.

Some children in professional families heard 450 different words and 210 questions in the three hours in which the parent spoke most. Another child in that same amount of time heard fewer than 200 different words and 38 questions. The results of the study led all to believe that the most important component of child care is the amount of talking occurring between child and caregiver.

But perhaps they were wrong. Newer research by Catherine Tamis-LeMonda of New York University and Marc Bornstein of the National Institutes of Health lead us down a slightly different path. When comparing maternal responsiveness in children who came from professional families, they found some surprises. The study found that the average child spoke his or her first words by thirteen months and by eighteen months had a vocabulary of about fifty words. However, mothers who were considered high responders, that is, they responded to their child's speech quickly and often, had children who were clearly six months ahead of the children whose mothers were low responders. These toddlers spoke their first words at ten months, had extensive vocabularies, and could speak in short sentences by fourteen months (Bronson & Merryman, 2009).

This response pattern sent specific messages to the brains of the toddlers. The first message is that what they are saying makes a difference and causes a reaction. In other words, what they are saying is important. The second message the brain receives is that objects and sounds have a connection. Words are not just words; they name things. In this newer study, the findings were based not on economic factors, only on the type of response given. The research by Patricia Kuhl (2007) from the University of Washington suggests that interaction is a crucial component of learning language, and therefore babies need an audience. Michael Goldstein in his B.A.B.Y. lab at Cornell University proved this. He performed a study in which babies were put in denim overalls that contained wireless microphones. Mother and baby were put in a room, and the mother was told simply to play with her baby. She was not to speak to her child, but was told to respond in an affectionate way by smiling and touching. The babies' babbling went from weak and very nasal to a stronger babbling that included consonant and vowel sounds (Goldstein, Bornstein, Schwade, Baldwin, & Brandstadter, 2007). The conclusion was that responding in a positive way to the babbling had a strong effect.

Windows of Opportunity

The concept of windows of opportunity, or critical periods, as some call them, refers to the time when the brain is developing in a specific area. It is thought that if a child is not exposed to stimuli to encourage that development, the window may close and the baby might not learn the skills associated with that development. For example, it is important that babies hear the sounds of their language or any other language they will be hearing or speaking within the first seven to eleven months of life.

Physically the brain shows change in several ways. First, more brain wave activity can be observed in an area of the brain if it is hooked up to an electroencephalogram, which measures the amount of electrical current present in the various areas. Second, the brain may be found to have more myelin, the white fatty substance that coats neuron axons, the nerve fibers that send information. Myelination offers faster and easier transmission of messages. Third, there may be dendritic growth found in specialized areas. Dendrites are the appendages of the neuron that receive information. More dendrites indicate more uses for that neuron. Finally, synaptic density may increase. Synapses are the spaces between neurons that are necessary for communication between the cells. Some or all of these may be present during these open window periods. Table 1.2 shows the windows of opportunity or critical periods associated with certain developmental milestones.

Experience and Brain Development

With the development of specialized structures in the brain over the first few months of life, babies begin to make sounds that will develop into syllables and then words. It takes the development of many critical areas for the baby to go from being a passive receiver to active participant in conversation.

Experience is key to proper language development. A child's environment and experiences will wire up the brain for a distinct language or languages. So although we know that most infants follow the same schedule for language, each individual life experience makes one child's development different from another's (Sleeper, 2007). If Maeve had been taken from her English-speaking parents and adopted by a family in China, she would just as easily have learned Chinese as she would have learned English. If she was

Table 1.2 Windows of Opportunity for Learning

Type of Learning	Window Opens	Window Narrows
Auditory development	At about four and a half months in utero, the fetus begins to hear sounds. By six months in utero, the fetus can hear voices and shortly after can recognize voices.	Ages eight to ten
First-language development	Birth	Ages ten to twelve
Emotional development	Birth	Continues throughout life
Math development	Birth	Continues throughout life
Music development	Responds to music in utero	Continues throughout life
Memory development	Birth	Continues throughout life
Second-language development	Birth	Continues throughout life; the earlier the better
Visual development	Birth	Critical in the first few months

raised in an environment in which little conversation took place and her primary caregiver did not speak to her, this experience would have a negative effect on her language development and the schedule that is usually followed by the brain for most babies.

The child who is strapped in a car seat and left in a room void of conversation and interaction for the first year or two of life will suffer in many ways, including delayed speech and motor development. Cases of this type of abuse are rare, but they have taught us much about language development. One such case is the famous situation of a girl called Genie (not her real name). Locked in a room and tied to a potty chair by her psychotic father, Genie wasn't discovered until she was thirteen years old. As a result of her isolation, her language development was arrested. A genie is a creature who comes out of a bottle as an adult, someone who didn't have a normal human childhood. This young girl fit that description. She wasn't locked in the room until she was close to two years old, so she had developed some infantile language before she was removed from much human contact. When she was found and given attention and teaching, she developed a large vocabulary of nouns and verbs, but she never had the ability to put complete sentences together because her brain was deprived during a critical period (James, 2008).

Ages and Stages in Language Development

"Parentese," the singsong language that is associated with the way most parents speak to their babies, is an important component of language development. This form of speaking keeps the baby's attention, and since it drags out sounds and syllables, it is easier for the brain to clearly hear and differentiate sounds—for example, "Mommy is going to snap your sleeper. Onnne, Twoooo, Threee, Fourrrr. Snap!" (Tallal, 2007).

Here is a brief outline of the stages that children typically go through in developing language:

- *From birth through three months:* Babies begin to coo and make sounds that are similar to vowel sounds. The brain is being stimulated to grow new dendrites and synapses as the baby is exposed to the sounds of language and other noises (Eliot, 2006).

- *From three to six months:* Babies begin to make "raspberry" sounds as they play with their language, and babbling becomes a frequent pastime. They copy the tones and cadence of their primary caregivers, and their vocalizing begins to sound conversational. The baby's vision and speech will progress as the occipital and parietal lobes develop. The occipital lobe stores words as pictures, and the parietal lobe integrates all sensory information, which assists the child in understanding words in an auditory, visual, and tactile way. As the baby sees more clearly, he may try to shape his mouth to match that of the person speaking to him (Stamm, 2007).

- *From six to nine months:* Parentese can be very important at this stage of development as babies begin to imitate the sounds they hear. Their language pathways have been mapped, and the brain continues to strengthen those connections as the baby listens and practices making those sounds.

- *From nine to twelve months:* Babies begin to respond to varied tones of voice, and their memory increases as the hippocampus (the structure in the brain that helps us form long-term memories) is developing. The ability to remember words and understand their meanings increases. Actual speech may begin at this age (Sprenger, 2008). The ability to segment speech (divide words into their sounds) begins at approximately nine months.

- *From twelve to eighteen months:* As the prefrontal lobe (the part of the frontal lobe where higher-level thinking is done) develops, babies begin to think more logically, understand and use gestures, and often follow simple directions. With a clearer understanding of words, they can label objects or point to them as they are named (Christie, Enz, & Vukelich, 2007).

- *From eighteen to twenty-four months:* The toddler may put simple sentences together and sing simple songs, although some words may be unclear to listeners. Language and vocabulary begin exploding as children add an average of eight or nine words per day. The brain begins using more energy, and the baby's brain has twice the number of connections as an adult brain does (Stamm, 2007). There are so many connections because toddlers are learning more than they will retain. Eventually many of those connections will be pruned away as they begin to use only the connections most important to their lives.

- *From twenty-four to thirty-six months:* More blood flow is seen in the left hemisphere of the brain where speech centers are located, signifying more activity in this area as more energy is burned. Vocabulary increases to as many as one thousand words. Sentence structure improves, and sentences contain more words.

- *From ages four to five:* Pretend play becomes even more important as children grasp language at higher levels. According to Laura Berk (2001), a child development expert, pretend play and talking to peers during this play have been positively associated with the size of a child's vocabulary by the age of five.

An Enriched Environment for Language Development

A child's ability to read is greatly influenced by his or her language development. Just as young Genie had her ability to speak and understand greatly inhibited by her early environment, most children thrive in their surroundings and follow the speech schedule easily.

Is there a difference between a normal environment and an enriched environment when it comes to speech? Obviously

Genie's environment was what Marian Diamond (1997) and other neuroscientists would call impoverished. To see what would constitute the best environment in which children can learn their primary language, compare the following four-year-old children:

• Mia appears to have everything a child could want. Her playroom is filled with blocks, clay, dolls, trucks, and balls. She has both a sand table and a water table. Her play kitchen is in the corner of the room, and she loves to serve food to her guests. When she finishes cooking, she washes and dries her dishes. When Mia's daddy comes home from work, they play. She loves to be an airplane, so Daddy lies on the floor and lifts Mia into the air on the soles of his feet. She giggles when Daddy "lands" her on the nearby sofa. Mia is a happy child. When she is tucked in at night, she looks forward to the next day.

• Sam loves to play with trucks. He has about twenty different kinds of trucks that he lines up on the shelf, plays with, and pushes around his room while making loud truck noises. Besides his trucks, Sam loves his train table. He has a conductor's hat, bandana, and train whistle. He yells, "All aboard," and then chugs his train around the track. At night, Sam's parents read him train books. He especially likes *The Little Engine That Could* and *Thomas Wins the Race.*

• Alaska's parents both work. Her mom works at home as a virtual assistant. She does bookkeeping, answers e-mails, and plans meetings for her employer. It takes her hours to complete her daily assignments, and she often works until late in the evening. As she works on the computer, she has little time for Alaska or her siblings. When Alaska's dad comes home from work, he kisses his family hello and sits down in front of the television. Alaska often tries to sit with her dad, but there is little communication between them. Often he just tells her, "Go play," or, "Quit bothering me."

Fortunately the house is well babyproofed and Alaska is safe. Mom stops her work to make dinner for the family; however, while the children sit at the table to eat, Mom eats at the computer and Dad eats in front of the TV. Dad puts the kids to bed and reads them one story before he turns out the lights.

• When Jack was three days old, his mom started reading *Goodnight Moon* to him. He couldn't understand one word of the book and the pictures were fuzzy, but he fell in love with reading as he was cradled in his mother's arms feeling warm and cozy. The sound of her voice was soothing to little Jack, and the melodic way she read kept him mesmerized by the sounds. Every night until Jack was old enough to ask for a different book or additional books, he still heard *Goodnight Moon*. Throughout the day, Mommy and Daddy read different books to him, and he grew to love the power and the stories that came from words. When Jack plays in his kitchen, he comes up to visitors with a pad and a crayon to take their order. He pretends to write down what they want and is forthright in telling his customers that he doesn't have certain items. He and Daddy decided to make a menu that Jack could post so his guests would not order anything "not on the menu." Jack dictated to his father as he wrote the menu. Jack "wrote" a few words on the menu to personalize it.

Of these children, Alaska receives the least amount of attention and interaction. Mia is happy and has conversations at home, but there is little reading. Sam's environment is good because he is read to and has lots of time for imaginative play, but Jack comes from the most literacy-rich home. His experiences include language, and his parents started him on the road to reading from birth. The sounds of language, the use of language, and even pretending about language all help a child to love communication and eventually love reading.

According to the American Academy of Pediatrics (2005), children need the following elements in their environment in order to reach full potential:

- To feel special
- To feel loved
- To feel safe
- To know what is going to happen (predictability)
- To have guidance
- To have a balance between freedom and limitations
- To be exposed to:
  - Language
  - Play
  - Exploration
  - Books
  - Music

Language and Gender

Gender differences have long been studied in many areas of cognitive development, and researchers have found that boys tend to be about a year and a half behind girls in reading and writing (Gurian, 2007). Boys are at a disadvantage for several reasons: they mature more slowly than girls, they are ill (and absent from school) more often, sometimes their fine motor skills have a slower start, their mastery of language is slower, and they may have self-control issues.

Research suggests, in fact, that boys may be at an extreme disadvantage compared with girls. Most of the major learning and developmental disorders—including dyslexia, autism, and attention deficit disorder—are found four times as often in boys than in girls (Eliot, 2009). Let's start at the beginning.

Most babies are born with twenty-three pairs of chromosomes, with each pair consisting of one chromosome from Dad and one from Mom. The two chromosomes in each of the first twenty-two look very similar to each other and contain the same genes. If one of the genes on a chromosome is defective, the other chromosome will send genetic material to it in order to fix it. If this is unsuccessful, the perfect chromosome takes over the responsibility for the task of that gene, and the other chromosome in the pair becomes inactive and is sometimes said to "hibernate."

For instance, if the number ten chromosome that I received from my father has a defect, my number ten from my mother will try to fix it. Mom's been trying to fix Dad for years, and of course, it doesn't work. So Mom's chromosome takes over and Dad's hibernates, and the defect does not affect me. It sounds like a great plan, and it works very well in most cases; however, if both chromosomes have the same defect, the imperfection is expressed.

When it comes to the twenty-third pair of chromosomes, life is different because these chromosomes determine gender. If you are a male, you receive a Y chromosome from your dad and an X from your mom. The father's chromosome always determines the sex of a child by providing an X or a Y. Mom always provides an X. Xs and Ys have very few genes in common. Since the Human Genome Project identified the genes on our chromosomes, scientists now know that many of the almost two thousand genes on the X involve brain function. A female has the luxury of a backup X if there are any defects on one of them. Males do not have that comfort. From verbal skills to socialization, a damaged gene on the X chromosome can be debilitating to males. Females actually use only one of their Xs, as too much of a good thing is not a good thing, and so the second X is deactivated at least partially very early in brain development (Medina, 2008). Therefore, the female brain acts much like the male brain. The male brain may be subject to more cognitive disorders, schizophrenia, or autism if the X chromosome has defects.

What about speech and reading? Could there be an effect if a boy's X chromosome is damaged? Researchers in the United Kingdom analyzed several studies and came to the following conclusion: boys have more reading problems than girls (Clark & Burke, 2012). Although this conclusion has also been debated, it appears to make sense: since boy brains and girl brains are different from the beginning, the approach they take toward speech and language may also vary.

Speaking Out of Both Sides of the Brain

The first class on the brain that I took, in the 1980s, was called Left Brain/Right Brain. In that class I was told that 80 percent of all men were "left brained" and 80 percent of women were "right brained." The explanation hinged on the fact that the left hemisphere was thought to be more linear, sequential, detail oriented, and focused on one thing at a time, and it controlled feelings. The right hemisphere was considered to be focused on the big picture and be more creative, intuitive, and free with feelings. The female brain was too emotional; the male brain lacked emotion.

As the 1980s progressed, the right brain/left brain theory fell by the wayside as brain research moved on because certainly everyone is whole brained. Surely science could look at the brain in a more productive way. There are differences in the male and female brain; however, they are not so cut-and-dried as right brain/left brain. When it comes to language and reading, it is necessary to take another look at the two hemispheres. Some researchers suggest that the female brain is more left-hemisphere-oriented during the first few years, and that is why baby girls are more verbal. They also suggest that the male brain has more activity in the right hemisphere, which may account for little boys being more spatially oriented and less verbal than girls (Gurian, Henley, & Trueman, 2001).

The hemispheres work together, but in early development, blood flow and electrical activity can be observed in one hemisphere, in both hemispheres, and cross talk between them. This cross talk is not interference; it is actually a communication in which one hemisphere does its job and then information flows to the other hemisphere to function in another way.

The information flows through the band of fibers called the corpus callosum. This structure is immature at birth, and its growth is encouraged through the communication of the hemispheres. Think of the corpus callosum as a path in the woods that has not yet been traveled enough to have the weeds and debris removed. When you travel this path, you must push the branches of bushes aside and perhaps kick away a few rocks. The more the path is used, the smoother it becomes.

Kusche and Greenberg (2006) discuss the earliest opportunities for the hemispheres to connect, which is through emotional experiences. Before a baby has learned language, the caregiver needs to supply the words. It begins simply: "See the doll," or, "This is your nose." Words need to be provided for experiences as well. For instance, when Maeve falls down as she tries to reach for something, she may cry. Her parents have the choice of saying, "You're okay. You'll be fine," and then help her get up if she cannot do it herself. If, however, they talk about her feelings, both emotional and physical, they can provide an opportunity for the hemispheres to begin connecting. If they say, "I'm sorry you hurt yourself. Let me kiss your elbow. You must be sad that you fell and couldn't reach your teddy bear," they are giving Maeve words that are processed by her left hemisphere and then offer feelings that are processed by the right hemisphere. The path between the two has begun to be laid.

Table 1.3 Functions of the Hemispheres

Left Hemisphere	Right Hemisphere
Detail oriented	Big picture
Sequential	Holistic
Contains speech centers in most humans: expressive and receptive language, speech, grammar, sounds	Prosody and tone of language
	Sensory image memory
	Sends unpleasurable emotional signals
Verbal short-term memory	Receives both pleasant and unpleasant feelings
Pleasurable emotion	
Facts	Reads body language and facial expression
Abstract processing	Concrete processing
Knowledge	Emotional significance of knowledge

Why is this important to language? Table 1.3 shows the functions of each hemisphere. Words and word meanings, for example, are processed in the left hemisphere, but tone and prosody (the pitch, tone, and rhythm of speech), as well as the emotional components of language, are processed in the right. The earlier the brain can begin developing those connections between hemispheres, the easier it will be for the child to understand language, meanings, and words (Kagan & Herschkowitz, 2005).

Activities

There are many ways in which both parents and teachers can encourage the development of language. Before children are in a formal school setting, the child's primary caregivers are her first teacher.

Ages Birth to Two

•   Talk to the child. Explain what you are doing as you do it: "There are three snaps on your jacket . . . one, two, three!"

Mirror Neurons

One of the most exciting discoveries in the brain sciences in the past decade has been that of mirror neurons. If you ever wonder why you yawn when you see someone else do it, mirror neurons are the reason. These brain cells mirror the connections going on in the brain of those you watch and listen to.

In 1995, quite inadvertently, some researchers in Italy were monitoring what was going on in the brains of monkeys as they reached for something (Iacoboni, 2009). A researcher mimicked the monkeys' movements while one was watching, and the response of the neural activity in the monkey's brain was the same as if it were making the movement.

Mirror neurons activate when we watch an action and when we read about it. In learning a language, this stresses the importance of children interacting with others and seeing their facial, mouth, and tongue movements in order to mimic them. A newborn will actually stick out her tongue if the adult holding her is sticking out his. Researchers like Marco Iacoboni, author of *Mirroring People* (2009), believe that a network of mirror neurons plays a role in humans' capacity to learn through imitation, use semantics in language, and feel empathy. When parents and teachers express themselves clearly and respond to the child's attempts at conversation with happy or exciting facial expressions, those mirror neurons respond and feel joy as well. Watching as parents show joy in reading, and especially reading aloud to the child, may also give the child joy and possibly encourage more listening and learning to read.

- Acknowledge and repeat back to the baby any sounds he makes.

- Imitate the baby's facial expressions, and overexaggerate yours. For instance, play peek-a-boo and show an exaggerated surprised look.

- Read aloud to your baby.

- Let your baby look in the mirror and see his mouth as he makes sounds. Make sure he sees your mouth as you talk to him.

Ages Two to Four

- Repeat what your child says so she knows you understand her.
- Read to your child.
- Name things: body parts, objects in the room, and so on.
- Pick up familiar items, and ask your child what they are.
- Sing nursery rhymes and songs. Encourage the child to sing along.
- Show the child photographs, and ask what is happening in them, or ask the child to tell a story about the picture.

Ages Four to Six

- Make sure you have the child's attention before you speak.
- Find objects to sort.
- Pause when you are speaking to give the child a chance to speak too.
- Give simple directions, and see if the child can follow them.
- Read aloud to the child.
- Play pretend games such as house.
- Take the child shopping and discuss what is on your list and the quantity. Have your child count out items for you.

From Six On

- Talk to your child.
- Read to your child.

Summary

Language is a human ability beyond comparison. It is hard-wired in the brain, so there are specific language areas already in place and waiting for the right experiences to help them connect. With the proper environment and with the knowledge gleaned from brain research, children can become better language learners. They can increase their vocabularies and their comprehension of words, so by the time they are ready to read, they understand that sound combinations can have meaning and affect their lives.

New research, however, suggests that there is no prewired pathway in the brain for reading. In the next chapter, we see that reading occurs through the recycling of neurons, in which brain cells are recruited to create a reading pathway, mainly from the language pathway. Therefore, it behooves all involved in the reading success of a child to ensure that the language pathway reaches its peak of productivity. The stronger the language pathway, the easier it will be for the brain to reuse some of those cells to create a strong reading network in the brain.

CHAPTER 2

Imaging and Imagining the Brain

I T IS ONLY THROUGH POWERFUL IMAGING techniques that we know so much about how the brain functions for learning. Researchers who are interested in how the brain learns to read rely heavily on these brain imaging machines to compare theories, compare readers, and discover what is not happening in the brains of those struggling to read. In the past, researchers dissected the brains of those who had reading difficulties after they passed away, in order to see what areas may have had lesions or where connections were lacking. Seeing the brain in action is what has made the difference for many of the students we see struggling today.

The ability to read is an expectation that we all have for our own children as well as everyone else's. Early childhood teachers expect to teach students to read. Intermediate, middle, and high school teachers expect students to be ready to read to learn. Living up to those expectations is a monumental task for many students. Children with reading problems feel ashamed, just as their parents and teachers feel guilty and ask themselves whenever a child fails to learn to read, "What did I do wrong? What should I have done? What can I do now to make it better?"

In this chapter, we look at how the brain works in order to lay the groundwork for understanding how children learn to read. If you are already familiar with some of this information, skip over sections. Especially if you are unfamiliar with the brain, this next section will provide you with the background knowledge you need to understand the most recent explorations of neuroscientists into the reading brain. The reading brain doesn't just automatically exist; it has to be created. Some call it a recycling process that occurs to make a brain a reading brain. Others simply call it a miracle.

The Structure of the Brain

An understanding of how reading development occurs is based on some basic knowledge of the brain's structure and function. The human brain has developed to adapt to a myriad possible environments in order for the species to survive. Throughout our lives, our brain will put the goal of our survival above all others. It drives the way we think, the way we act, and the way we avoid or pursue people, places, things, and ideas.

The adult brain weighs about three pounds. Male brains are generally heavier than female brains; however, this does not affect intelligence. At birth, the brain weighs only one pound. At that point, it is the least developed organ, but it has already begun to develop connections for both smell and sound. It is divided into two halves, or hemispheres, which are connected by a band of fibers called the corpus callosum. The functions of the two hemispheres are key in observing how the development of the brain and language occur. Keep in mind, however, that these hemispheres work together, and we are all "whole-brained." In fact, the concept of left-brained or right-brained people has become obsolete.

The outer layer of the brain is called the neocortex. This layer, which is anywhere from $1/8$- to $1/4$-inch thick, is the part of the brain that makes us uniquely human. It is here that our higher-level thinking occurs.

Each of the two hemispheres of the brain is divided into four lobes: the temporal, frontal, parietal, and occipital lobes (see figure 2.1) The figure also includes two speech centers that will be discussed shortly.

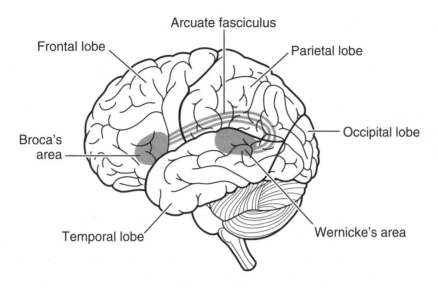

❖❖ FIGURE 2.1: *Lobes of the Brain and the Two Speech Centers. The band of fibers connecting Broca's area and Wernicke's area is called the arcuate fasciculus.*

The interaction of these lobes, along with some specific language centers, leads us to a basic understanding of how spoken language, and eventually reading, occurs.

Occipital Lobes

These lobes are located at the back of the brain. If you take your hand and place it directly on the back of your head, you will be millimeters away from these lobes. It is here that visual information is recognized and interpreted. The outer layer of neocortex covering the occipital lobes is the visual cortex, one of the important areas for reading.

Parietal Lobes

Located above the occipital lobes and at the top of the back of the brain, the parietal lobes integrate sensory information. A vital structure for reading, these lobes combine tactile input with both sounds and visual information entering the brain.

Temporal Lobes

Above your ears and on either side of your brain lie your temporal lobes. Responsible for hearing, some speech, and some memory, these lobes are covered by the part of the neocortex called the auditory cortex. Incoming auditory stimuli are interpreted by these lobes.

Frontal Lobes

Behind your forehead is the prefrontal cortex, which is part of the frontal lobes. These lobes are in charge of reasoning, motor skills, higher-level cognition, and expressive language. The part of the neocortex that covers the frontal lobes is known as the association cortex. It is in the frontal lobes that decisions are made by drawing on prior memories and adding some emotional information from the amygdala, the structure responsible for our raw emotions. The frontal lobes, sometimes called the CEO of the brain, aid us in controlling our emotions, so we don't always act on them. (You may feel like pushing the person who just cut ahead of you in line, but your frontal lobes help you control that desire.)

Thalamus

This is sometimes referred to as "Grand Central Station" for the brain. The thalamus receives all incoming information and sends it to the appropriate areas for processing. For instance, auditory information is sent to the auditory cortex and visual information to the visual cortex.

Broca's Area

Paul Broca (1824–1880), a French surgeon, named this area when he encountered a patient who understood but could not express language. On autopsy, Broca found damage in the left frontal lobe. Articulation of speech and comprehension of meaning are two of the functions of this area.

Wernicke's Area

Discovered by Carl Wernicke (1848–1904), a German psychiatrist who dissected the brains of two men who were unable to understand language or create coherent speech, this region, located in the left temporal lobe and adjacent to the parietal lobe, is used for comprehending language. Both spoken and written words as well as sign language activate this area. This is your mental lexicon, your brain's dictionary.

Arcuate Fasciculus

This is the band of fibers that connect Broca's area and Wernicke's area and relay information between these two structures.

Angular Gyrus

This cortical structure lies between Wernicke's area and the visual cortex, the outer layer of the occipital lobe. It is responsible for recognizing symbols such as letters.

Cerebellum

This brain structure is located in the back of the brain beneath the occipital lobe. Often called the "little brain," the cerebellum helps with the timing and synchronization of speech.

How We See the Brain

Although information about brain structure and function used to be found only through surgery or on autopsy, brain imaging techniques now allow neuroscientists and medical professionals to view and analyze the brain. Some brain imaging requires exposure to radiation, but many more techniques do not.

From X-rays to more recent imaging techniques, the brain can be seen in many formats. Depending on what scientists or clinicians are measuring, they now commonly use a half-dozen scanning devices, and there are more on the horizon.

Following are some of the most useful tools for discovering how the brain looks and functions.

Electroencephalography

Brain function is both electrical and chemical. Electroencephalography (EEG) measures the electrical activity in the brain. It helps scientists see when there are areas of neurons that respond to specific stimuli. When sensors are placed on the scalp, electrical oscillations or cycles in the brain during specific tasks, such as speaking or reading, can be graphed.

Computerized Axial Tomography

Computerized axial tomography, sometimes called a CT (or CAT) scan, combines X-rays with computer technology to produce two- and three-dimensional images of slices of the brain. These scans show the structure but not the function of the brain. Also, because radioactivity is required in producing these scans, it is not the imaging technique of choice when examining the brain for purposes of educational research.

Positron Emission Tomography

Positron emission tomography (PET) measures the amount of radiation and activity in various brain areas. The brain runs on glucose, so subjects are injected with radioactive glucose that can be traced as it circulates in the brain. Areas that are more active require more glucose, so researchers watch a computer screen to see which areas produce more blood flow, which indicates more glucose in those areas, during tasks such as speaking and reading (Sousa, 2010). On the screen, reds and yellows indicate the most activity.

Although PET was the first imaging technique to show how the brain functions, it is not used as much now as it was in the past because of the need to use radiation and inject the subject. PET scans are generally not done on children unless a physical problem in the brain is suspected.

The scans in figure 2.2, for example, tell us quite a story. Individuals in the scanning machine were asked to do some tasks related to reading, and we can see on the scans where brain connections necessary for reading are being used.

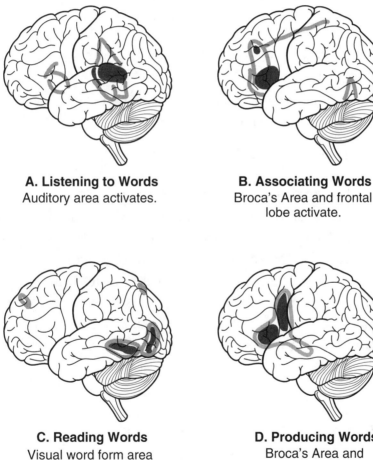

A. Listening to Words
Auditory area activates.

B. Associating Words
Broca's Area and frontal
lobe activate.

C. Reading Words
Visual word form area
and visual cortex active.

D. Producing Words
Broca's Area and
motor cortex active.

❖ FIGURE 2.2: *Areas Activated in the Brain by Skills Associated with Reading.*

Discoveries Through Brain Imaging

Among the discoveries about reading that have been made using these brain imaging tools are these:

- Struggling readers have brains that are working harder than those of nonstruggling readers.
- Readers with dyslexia are using different areas of their brains than fluent readers are.
- Novice readers use different paths in the brain from those who are expert or skilled readers.
- Various intervention methods can rewire the brains of some struggling readers and dyslexic readers for reading.

Functional Magnetic Resonance Imaging

Functional magnetic resonance imaging (fMRI) shows researchers the levels of deoxygenated blood in brain cells. As the subject thinks, the brain areas require oxygen and glucose for this task. Oxygen is transported to the neurons via hemoglobin. The iron in hemoglobin reacts to a large magnet that is used in the procedure. In this way, scientists are able to compare the amount of blood entering and leaving the brain cells, showing them which areas are the most active.

Brain Cells

All brain structures are made up of individualized cells. Some of these cells communicate with others to create networks that help us learn and remember. Other cells are nurturing cells that care for the needs of learning cells.

Neurons

Estimates are that each of us is born with 100 billion neurons—the cells that learn. In utero, a fetus has up to 200 billion neurons, but half are gone before birth. The brain creates these extra neurons to enhance survival and prunes away those that are not needed. In its characteristic "use it or lose it" manner, neurons that are or will be used are spared. Neurons do not generally regenerate. Therefore, you lose cells that may not be replaced. However, scientists have found that in some areas of the brain, new cells are generated (Doidge, 2007). These areas include the hippocampus, which is so important to learning: it is a seahorse-shaped structure in the middle of the brain that helps to form new memories,

These cells make up only 10 percent of the brain; they are small enough that thirty thousand of them can fit on the head of a pin! Neurons can be divided into three basic parts: the cell body, dendrites, and axons. The cell body contains a nucleus that consists of DNA, RNA, mitochondria, and other substances to sustain the cell and aid in either remembering or forgetting. Dendrites that grow from the cell body as the neuron learns receive information from other cells. As more information is learned, more dendrites grow. Each of the neurons in your brain has between six thousand and ten thousand dendrites, which allow them to connect to between six thousand and ten thousand other neurons. A neuron may have many dendrites, but it has one only appendage, an axon, which sends information out to other cells. Although a neuron is a singular structure, it grows small attachments called axon terminals as the demand in the number of messages to be sent increases. (See figure 2.3.)

Most axons are coated with a sheath of a white lipid, or fat, called myelin. There is still some debate about the schedule of myelination. Some researchers believe that myelin is formed as the neurons are used. As the neuron connects more with other neurons, the transmission encourages myelin formation. The myelin consists

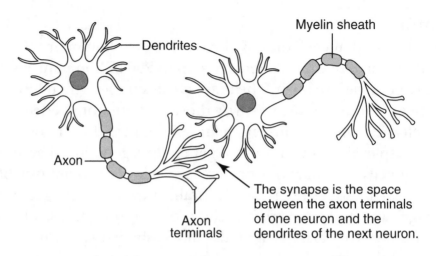

Myelin sheath

Dendrites

Axon

Axon terminals

The synapse is the space between the axon terminals of one neuron and the dendrites of the next neuron.

FIGURE 2.3: *How Information Flows. Information flows in through the dendrites and out through the axon.*

of cells called oligodendricytes that wrap themselves around the axon. These are a type of nurturing cell whose mission is to protect and enhance the transmission of information. Other researchers state that myelin formation is determined by brain development itself. As certain areas of the brain develop, axons are coated with myelin to assist in their work.

Everything we do, that is, every human behavior, is the result of neurons communicating with each other. Language, reading, and writing are a result of neurons communicating. Understanding how the brain functions at the cellular level aids in our understanding of what happens when a child reads easily and well and what may be going on in the brain of a struggling reader.

Glia

The nurturing cells are called glia or glial cells (*glia* is the Latin word for glue). There are several types of glia. Some make up the blood–brain barrier, a mechanism for varying the ability of some substances to pass into the brain and some to carry away waste material, such as dead neurons and leftover oxygen molecules.

The oligodendrocytes are glia that become the myelin coating on axons. Microglia are cells that clean away debris, such as parts of neurons that are no longer viable. Glial cells make up 90 percent of the brain and they do regenerate.

Recent research on the glial cells has presented interesting information as to what duties they perform. In the case of the oligodendrocytes, which wrap themselves around the axons as myelin, it is now thought that they take some action in the timing of the transmittal of messages (Leitzell, 2008).

How Cells Communicate

The transmission of messages in the brain is an electrical-chemical reaction. To understand how this works, you must know about two more components of nerve impulses: synapses and neuro-transmitters.

Synapses

Synapses are the spaces between the axon of a neuron and the dendrites of another neuron. Remember that information is sent out through the axon and received by the dendrite. In theory, communicating neurons don't touch each other. Inside the neuron, a message is electrical, but between neurons, the message is chemical. There is no electrical "wire" within the synapse between neurons. Instead, chemicals called neurotransmitters carry the messages across the synapse.

Neurotransmitters

When you learn something, a certain amount of chemical is released through the axon of one neuron and attaches itself to the dendrite(s) of another neuron. The second time that same connection is activated, the connection becomes stronger and less of the chemical is needed to make the connection. The next time it is activated, it takes even less of the chemical. Every time a chemical message is repeated, it is said to strengthen the synapse. This strengthening is referred to as long-term potentiation (LTP). Whenever children practice reading or other content, they are strengthening the synapse, or LTP, and creating memory. In simpler terms, reactivation of these connections increases the potential of these neurons to fire again and fire more quickly and easily, literally using less energy.

The proper balance of neurotransmitters keeps the brain running smoothly. When imbalances occur, such as from improper nutrition, lack of sleep, genetic changes, and stress, among other things, not only will there be difficulties in learning and memory, but also serious disorders such as schizophrenia may occur.

Although many neurotransmitters have been identified, only a handful are pertinent to the discussion in this book, and we examine them briefly next. They are involved in mood, transmitting messages, and in learning and memory.

Dopamine   Dopamine is one of the most important neurotransmitters. Extra dopamine is released when you feel pleasure. That positive emotion spurs on the release of other neurotransmitters as well. So when children find learning pleasurable, more chemicals are released that help to make faster connections and create more memories.

In the prefrontal cortex of the brain, dopamine is important to block out distractions. The lack of impulse control that we see in children with attention deficit hyperactivity disorder has been related to a lack of dopamine in this area. Again, pleasurable learning will help release more dopamine and make it easier for children to concentrate, control their impulses, and continue learning.

Norepinephrine   This neurotransmitter, which is involved in learning and memory, is needed to form new memories and transfer them to long-term storage sites. This excitatory neurotransmitter, one that causes neurons to make connections, is needed for motivation, concentration, and alertness.

Serotonin This chemical helps calm the brain and body and also affects appetite and body temperature. It regulates memory, for example. An insufficient supply of serotonin is known to be associated with aggression, depression, and insomnia.

Acetylcholine Acetylcholine is critical for both movement and memory. Some believe that one of the reasons movements associated with learning increase memory is due to the release of this neurotransmitter.

Gamma-Aminobutyric Acid (GABA) This chemical is associated with most of the transmission of messages in the brain. It is a calming chemical that keeps the brain from being overstimulated.

Glutamate This chemical stimulates and activates systems involved in learning and memory.

What We Thought We Knew

Research constantly changes our theories and beliefs, so finding the definitive answers to the questions we have seems an impossible task. As a reading teacher, I always wondered why a curriculum or a strategy worked for one child and not another. It didn't make sense until I learned more about the brain. It made even more sense as I learned more about the child—the whole child.

When my husband was a child and was having great difficulty in learning to read, the teachers thought they knew the reasons. They'd say, "He's lazy," "He's just not trying," "He's too active," "He's too inactive," "He needs to read more," or, "He needs to try harder.'' In those days teachers did what they thought was best: they had him read more. His mother listened to him read, his teacher listened to him read, and special reading teachers listened to him read. Although they corrected his mispronounced words, they didn't show him how to take those words apart and identify the sounds the letters made. They knew nothing about phonemic awareness. I truly believe in the words of Maya Angelou when she says, ''We did what we knew, and when we knew better, we did better.'' How Scott made it through school with any kind of self-esteem amazes me. He did, however, because he is extremely intelligent and had people around him who loved him and accepted him. He learned to compensate by memorizing enormous numbers of words, found identifying the gist of a reading quite helpful, and put his efforts into problem-solving and spatial skills. His teachers didn't know that. They just knew that they could ''send him on'' to the next teacher, leaving it to that person to deal with his lack of doing his reading and therefore his lack of comprehension.

I wish I could tell you that Scott found a magical teacher who knew how to help him and that's why he graduated from college, reads and understands technical language that is beyond me, and has had a wonderful and fulfilling career. But that wouldn't be true. Scott made it because he was smart enough to figure out how to survive in an environment that offered him little support. His brain was *that* good. It just wasn't a reading brain.

What We Found Out Along the Way

Through years of research, we now understand that although we knew practice was a good thing to help the brain learn, simply practicing was not going to help struggling readers. Research supports that the components of reading, which are discussed in chapters 4 through 8, must be explicitly taught. Phonemic awareness is not something that we are born able to do. If we follow the neuronal recycling theory, the only way to learn to read is to learn to use some of the visual neurons that are used for such things as faces, places, and objects to create the visual forms of words. We need to borrow a few neurons to create the ability to read.

As we look at the reading brain, keep in mind that the brain changes over time. Initially both hemispheres of the brain are active for speech and reading. But as the child ages, more left brain activity is noted in skilled readers. Struggling readers, however, will have brains that resemble younger brains that have not become skilled (Hoeft, 2010).

Learning to read requires that the word on the page translates into the sounds that you make or hear. Developing the language pathway makes it easier to rearrange neuronal connections to create the reading pathway.The ability to speak is about 4 million years old and is hard-wired in the brain. Reading, however, has been around for only four thousand years and is not hard-wired in the brain. There is no reading pathway in the brain at birth. But the brain has this wonderful language pathway (figure 2.4) that can be used for reading after some changes have been made. Stanislaw Dehaene (2009) calls this process *neuronal recycling.*

For the past two decades, images of the reading brain have shown results that follow a very linear pattern. Reading follows the language pathway (figure 2.5). Information entering the eye goes to the thalamus, a sort of relay station for incoming information, which sends the visual information to the visual cortex. From the visual cortex, information goes to the angular gyrus, where the print on the page is transformed into sounds, our phonemes. This is the key to fluent reading. From the angular gyrus, the information goes to Wernicke's area, our lexicon or dictionary, to find meaning. Then the information is sent to Broca's area via the arcuate fasciculus for phonological processing (reading).

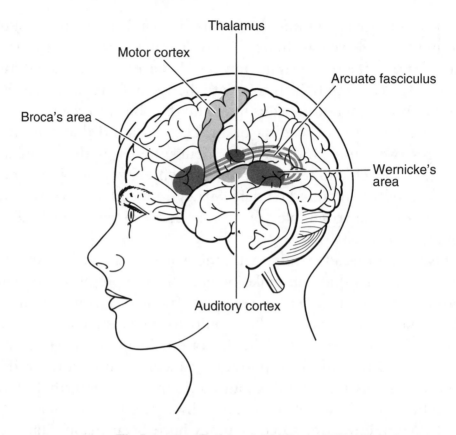

❖ FIGURE 2.4: *The Language Pathway in the Brain Is Hard-wired.*
Information in the form of sound comes into the ear. This information
is sent to an internal structure called the thalamus, which identifies the
information as auditory and sends it to the auditory cortex. From there,
the sounds are sent to Wernicke's area for identification. Via the
arcuate fasciculus, the information is transferred to Broca's area for
processing. Then the motor cortex becomes involved as the lips and
mouth prepare to speak.

Two Diverging Roads

Researchers such as Sally Shaywitz (2003) talk about two neural
pathways for reading, both residing on the left side of the brain.
The beginning reading pathway is higher up and called the parieto-
temporal; it is above the ear and slightly behind it. All beginning

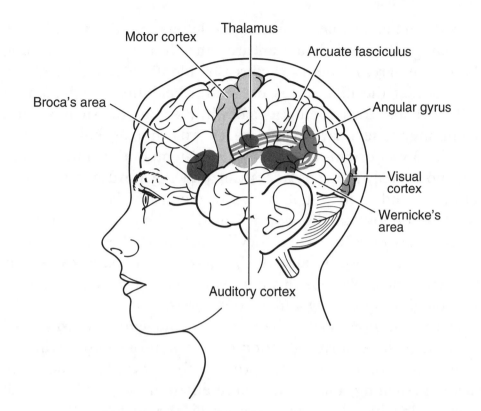

♦ FIGURE 2.5: *The Reading Pathway in the Brain Is Not Hard-wired.*
Information in the form of vision comes into the eye. This information
is sent to an internal structure called the thalamus. The thalamus
identifies the information as visual and sends it to the visual cortex.
From the visual cortex, the picture of the word is sent to Wernicke's area
for identification and comprehension via the arcuate fasciculus, and
the information is transferred to Broca's area for processing of syntax.
Then the information goes to the frontal lobes for comprehension.

readers use it for slowly sounding out words. More advanced readers
use the lower pathway, the occipito-temporal area. In this area, all
of the vital information about a word comes together to be stored
and can quickly be accessed. These readers use neural systems that
include regions in the back and on the left side of the brain for
processing the visual features of the letters, the visual cortex (lines,

curves), and areas that transform the letters into the sounds (the angular gyrus), and finally an area that has the word meaning (Wernicke's area). These structures are identified in figure 2.5.

A look at the differences between a beginning reader and a skilled reader offers a better idea of why there are two such systems. Beginning readers have to analyze a word, whereas skilled readers can identify a word instantly. The parieto-temporal region is slower and more analytical so readers can pull the word apart into its various sounds and put it back together to make the word. It basically sounds out the word. Skilled readers use the occipito-temporal area because when they see the word, they rapidly know the meaning. This is because the brain recognizes patterns—many different kinds. We look at patterns in chapter 5 as we examine phonological processing and word patterns.

Once beginning readers have read and analyzed a word several times, they have formed a network of neurons, stored in the occipito-temporal area, that represents that word. Pronunciation, meaning, spelling, and a visual representation for this word are all activated in a heartbeat, or automatically, the next time the reader sees the word. It is this reading pathway that we want all children to learn to use.

If good readers are compared to dyslexic readers using imaging devices, the differences of brain activation are plain to see. Good readers use the frontal lobe but show greater activity in the back of the brain; dyslexic readers show more activity in the frontal lobe and less at the back of the brain. As dyslexic readers grow, they show even more activation in the front of the brain. Asking struggling readers to "try harder" does nothing but put excessive stress on them. They are already working very hard to make sense of what they are reading. What they aren't doing is switching to the second pathway where words are instantly remembered. This difficult way to try to read brings in another area of concern for struggling readers: memory. If readers don't use the lower pathway in the brain where definitions, meanings, and spelling are practiced and remembered, then many struggling readers have few word memories. That is, they have a rather small mental lexicon in their brain. As we continue in this chapter and in others, we will see the important role memory plays in the reading process.

Developmentally, these pathways must be myelinated before they are mature enough to perform the reading process. Remember that myelin is the insulation covering the axons of most neurons. One of the structures that is so important to linking sounds and letters is the angular gyrus. Although most of the other structures are mature by the age of five, the angular gyrus may just be beginning to develop and mature (Wolf, 2008). In fact, it's possible that we are pushing reading on some student brains that are not yet ready to read.

Learning and Memory: A Definition

Learning is a process that begins at the neuronal level. It is the activation of neurons, possibly thousands of neurons, that are making connections in order to form neural networks. These networks are like maps in the brain. When you learned how to get from your home to your school, you created a picture in your mind of all of the streets and turns and possibly landmarks on your way. That picture that you can see of your driving path is a result of another map—a neural map that is making connections as you see the literal map in your mind. The first time you drove the route, you may have followed directions that were written or listened to the GPS in your car. The second time, you knew the route better. And now? Now you drive to school, and it is such an automatic procedure that you may wonder when you arrive how you got there.

Learning is the act of making connections between thousands of neurons that make up neural networks that must be strengthened through rehearsal. Memory then becomes the act of retrieving the stored information by reactivating them or reconstructing them.

We have many kinds of memory. To understand how we learn and remember, we next look at sensory memory, working memory, and long-term memory.

Sensory Memory

Sensory memory is the shortest type of memory. It is the ability to hold onto sensory information after it has stopped being transmitted. For instance, following a phone conversation, your memory of the auditory information disappears unless there was something important said that you wrote down or repeated to yourself. All information enters our brains through our senses. Our perception of the world comes in the form of visual (sight), auditory (sound), kinesthetic (touch), olfactory (smell), and gustatory (taste) information. This information is sent to appropriate areas called association cortices in the top layer of the brain, the cortex. It is here that information is identified. It would be impossible to pay attention to all incoming information, so unimportant information is dropped. In fact, up to 99 percent of sensory information is disregarded.

Working Memory

Working memory, sometimes called conscious memory, is the process by which the sensory memory is held in the brain. Psychologist and researcher George Miller, one of the founders of cognitive psychology and author of the often cited paper "The Magical Number Seven, Plus or Minus Two" (1956), did research in this area, and from his work it has long been thought that the power in this process allows us to hold up to seven pieces of information at one time (Baddeley, 1999). This work has been challenged, with the "magical number seven" reduced to four. According to some more recent studies, the brain has a more limited capacity in immediate memory than Miller proposed. Cowan (2001) concludes that adult capacity for short-term storage is between three and five pieces of information.

Working memory is the memory system we are constantly using. It can hold information "in mind" for minutes, hours, and even days and performs different tasks that are very important for school success, including the reading process. For example, seven-year-old Tyson is reading this sentence: "Germain was crying hysterically after the enormous dog jumped up against him." Tyson has never before seen the word *hysterically* and doesn't know how to pronounce it. He stops reading and looks at the word in silence hoping his teacher will tell him how to pronounce it. He waits several seconds with no results, so he tries to sound it out. His word attack skills are not that good, so he replaces the word with *hard*, because "crying hard" makes sense to him. He then continues the sentence and comes to the word *enormous*. Another long pause, and by the time he makes up a word to take the place of *enormous*, the sentence is not only changed, but Tyson has no recollection of what the first part of the sentence said.

Tyson didn't have enough working memory space to try to decode the words, make up new ones, and keep any of the text in mind simultaneously. His limited working memory space was filled up with his efforts. His memory space was also smaller than usual because this was a stressful situation and anxiety takes up some space as well.

As you read this book, keep in mind that the strategies involved with the components of reading are designed to enhance working memory. If a child has mastered the alphabetic principle, decodes words well, and is a fluent reader, working memory is free for the important job of comprehension.

Long-Term Memory
We can divide long-term memory into two categories: declarative and nondeclarative, or procedural. For reading, declarative is the "what" of reading and procedural memory is the "how."

Declarative Memory   Declarative memory is the memory for facts and events. It can be consciously retrieved and can be declared, that is, put into words. Semantic and episodic are the two memory systems in this category. Semantic memory refers to facts and concepts, and episodic memory includes our experiences, like time, places, people, and events. Declarative memory requires the use of the working memory processes, which involve several brain structures, including the hippocampus, which helps us form and store new memories (Bourtchouladze, 2002). Semantic memory contains the prior knowledge and the current text information so that it can be manipulated.

In terms of reading, semantic memory involves the use of Wernicke's area with the lexicon of words, Broca's area for the syntax and sentence structure, and the neocortex, which holds our prior knowledge. Comprehension of what we read involves our semantic memories.

Nondeclarative Memory   This memory system is the "how" of reading. It involves the decoding skills and the comprehension strategies that we teach to our students. Practice makes permanent. In the case of reading, decoding skills, learning sight and high-frequency words, fluency, some vocabulary, and the reading strategies that help us understand what we are reading all need to become part of procedural memory. In other words, they must become automatic in order to allow the brain the time and space it needs to comprehend text.

Summary

Understanding the brain's development, structure, and function reveals the reasons behind many of the struggles children face when they are unable to read and comprehend in the manner expected of them. As science continues to study and learn more about the brain and share those insights with educators, we get closer to translating the research into reading practices that can make a difference.

CHAPTER 3

The Body-Brain Connection

A T THREE MONTHS, MAEVE HAS JUST rolled over from front to back for the first time. Mom had put her on the floor for some tummy time, and Maeve would have none of that. She wanted to lie on her back to watch her big brother and sister. With some effort, she pulled up a knee, pushed up on her hands, and rocked herself onto her back.

Movement begins in the womb, as any mother can tell you. After birth, babies still have no control over their arms and legs, which often get in the way when feeding, dressing, and diapering them. But Maeve's accomplishment is a cause for celebration. Clapping and cheering mark this milestone, along with phone calls to grandparents and aunts and uncles. Maeve has little idea what this ruckus is about, but she appreciates the smiles and responds by kicking her legs and moving her arms. Soon she will roll over again and catch on to the fact that her new skill garners attention and should be repeated.

What Maeve doesn't know is that her physical skills will affect her cognitive abilities. Her movements are causing neurons to make connections, not only in the motor strip of her brain that has specific areas for feet, arms, and legs, as well as most of her other body parts, but throughout her brain (Hannaford, 2005).

The brain-body connection is not limited to movement. Everything we do affects our brain, including what we eat, how much we sleep, and how stressed our environment is. In this chapter, we examine some of the latest research findings and some suggestions from the experts to improve the quality of the body and the brain.

Food, Glorious Food!

Prenatal nutrition is an important part of brain development. For example, a lack of folic acid can cause a neural tube defect such as spina bifida. Folic acid, or vitamin B_9, is recommended for any woman who is pregnant or considering becoming pregnant. This substance is found in foods like green leafy vegetables and can also be taken as a vitamin supplement. In general, women who have healthy diets have a better chance of giving birth to a healthy baby whose brain has made the proper connections and is ready to learn about the outside world.

Another prenatal issue is alcohol. Alcohol consumption at critical stages in a fetus's brain development can cause fetal alcohol syndrome or fetal alcohol effect. The defects from these disorders affect mood, behavior, and cognition and memory. Many times the problem is that the neurons did not migrate to the appropriate areas in the brain. A neuron can morph into whatever type of cell that is needed. And as the brain develops and new neurons grow, they follow a pattern that takes them to the area of the brain where they are needed. For instance, visual neurons in blind babies can be used in other areas of the brain. But where alcohol changes the path of neurons, there are gaps in some brain structures and overcrowding in others.

The brain is only 2 percent of your total body weight, but it consumes 20 to 25 percent of its calories. Since it is the only organ that does not store energy, it must be constantly fed. Complex carbohydrates, which we get from fruits, vegetables, and grains, are preferred by the brain as a food source. The liver turns these into glucose, which travels up the carotid arteries to fuel the brain.

When we look at the consistency of the brain, it is composed of 78 percent water, 10 percent protein, and 10 percent fat. These are necessary components of any smart diet. The fats that are in the brain are omega-3 fatty acids. However, most of the fats in American foods are omega-6 fatty acids, which can cause clogging of arteries and allow less blood flow to the brain. So the body needs a combination of fats, especially omega-3. Omega-3 fats are called "essential fats": this means that the body and brain need them, but the body cannot produce them on its own, so we have to get them through food or supplements. The most common foods containing these essential fats are salmon, tuna, mackerel, olive oil, and sardines. Many physicians prescribe fish oil for their patients because it has been shown to lower cholesterol, prevent heart disease, and even improve joint health.

Neurotransmitters and Nutrition

You can think of every neuron in the brain as a manufacturing plant that receives nutrients and uses them to create neurotransmitters, the brain chemicals that help us in everything we do. Some neurotransmitters require the consumption of appropriate foods in order to be manufactured. Some of the foods are transformed into precursors of what the neurotransmitter needs, like the ingredients in a recipe.

The following list shows groups of food, the precursor they produce, the neurotransmitter that is manufactured, and the result in the brain:

- Proteins such as meats, eggs, cheese, fish, and nuts are used to produce tyrosine, which is used to manufacture the chemical dopamine. Dopamine assists with attention, focus, motivation, and a positive attitude.

- Turkey, milk, and some of the complex carbohydrates, such as whole grains, vegetables, and beans, are used to produce tryptophan, which then is used to manufacture serotonin. Serotonin affects mood, happiness, and relaxation.

- Liver, egg yolks, nuts, and soybeans contain the nutrients needed to produce choline, which is necessary for the production of acetylcholine. Acetylcholine affects the creation and retrieval of memory, movement, and concentration.

Depending on which neuroscientist you ask, between fifty and two hundred different neurotransmitters have been discovered in the brain. Not all of them rely so directly on specific types of foods; however, those I have listed are a few of the chemicals that do. And when you consider the results of a healthy balance of these chemicals in the brains of our children, wouldn't it seem much easier to teach students who came to classrooms each day with the proper diet?

10 Percent Protein

If your brain is 10 percent protein, doesn't it just make sense to supply your body and brain with some? Protein helps to form amino acids, building blocks for the brain. The neurotransmitter precursors tryptophan and tyrosine are amino acids. In order for young people to get the essential amino acids their brains need, protein must be part of their diet.

Amino acids can be absorbed from the bloodstream by the body's cells more easily than the brain can get them. This is mainly because they have to pass through the blood–brain barrier, which slows the process. The blood–brain barrier keeps unwanted molecules in the blood from entering the brain easily because it is semipermeable. Therefore, it is important to consume plenty of protein to make enough available for both brain and body. Meats, cheese, eggs, poultry, and yogurt provide many essential amino acids; for vegetarians, rice, beans, and grains can also combine to create the necessary amino acids and proteins for a complete diet.

Your Brain on Chocolate

If that title just made your mouth water and your mind wander, I apologize. We all know there is good news and bad news about this food. I am reminded of a television commercial in which someone is mountain climbing and seems to be too worn out to make it to the peak. A fellow climber reaches into his knapsack and pulls out a popular chocolate bar. The weary climber takes a bite of the candy and is quickly racing to the top of the mountain completely refreshed and happy.

So what's all that about? If you need a quick rush of brain activity, raw sugar like that will do it, but only temporarily. Then things get (forgive the pun) a little sticky. A short while later, if we were to check out the climber, he could be falling down the mountain! The surge of energy from simple carbohydrates raises blood sugar levels quickly, and almost just as quickly, those levels plummet, leaving the body tired, weak, and possibly shaky and irritable. Complex carbohydrates, however, raise blood sugar and insulin levels slowly and steadily, allowing you to concentrate and feel less hungry and less irritable (Augustine, 2007).

If you're miffed that I just took your chocolate candy, cakes, and cookies away from your healthy treat list, look at the good news when it comes to chocolate: *dark* chocolate is okay. Dark chocolate is full of antioxidants, and antioxidants are good for your brain and your body. They absorb the free radicals you may have read about. Those free radicals in the brain are left-over oxygen molecules that are as good for our brains as exposure to air is to a peeled apple. The apple gets brown. Imagine what happens in your brain! Don't like dark chocolate? Try different brands. You may find something you like. You can have a little bit daily.

They Are What They Eat!

When you look at Adam, you might miss his bright blue eyes because the dark circles under them attract your vision. He is pale much of the time, and his nose is forever running. When I spoke to Adam's mother about his dark circles, she simply remarked, "Oh, he takes after me. I always have dark circles under my eyes." She explained the runny nose by "seasonal allergies."

But no matter how many excuses Adam's mom had, clearly something else was going on with Adam. Not only did he look unwell, his behavior was quite unpredictable, and this was affecting his grades as well. When Adam's grades started to plummet, his mother became more interested in what could be done. She suggested extra homework, staying after school for me to tutor him, and private tutoring. This well-intentioned mom wanted to fix the results of the problem rather than the problem itself. If Adam had a food or environmental allergy that was causing the problem, extra work or tutoring was not going to solve the problem.

Doris Rapp, author of *Is This Your Child's World? How Schools and Homes Are Making Our Children Sick* (1997), suggests that parents have their children see an allergist to find out specifics if there is a learning problem. She also offers a quick test if a particular food is thought to be problematic. Ask the child to write her name. Then give her some of the food that is suspect. Wait for forty-five minutes, and ask the child to write her name again. Then compare the signatures. If the second signature is noticeably less legible than the first, you may have found part of the problem. Of course, the child must see a physician or allergist to confirm whether this is the case (Healy, 2010).

Adam's mother finally tried this simple test and found after some trial and error that Adam was sensitive to milk products. Once she substituted cow's milk with soy, his eyes became bright and clear, and that nose finally stopped running. Feeling better helped him focus and attend to learning. He had some catching up to do, but that became an easier task now. Adam was fortunate that his problem could be easily diagnosed. We cannot expect easy solutions. The point is to get to the root of the problem and not just work on the symptoms.

When They Eat

The timing of eating can also affect behavior, mood, and learning. One example is skipping breakfast. Since the brain doesn't store energy, it's running on fumes when a child awakens in the morning. Breakfast is the most important meal of the day.

Why do people skip breakfast? Here are some typical excuses parents and teachers hear:

- "I'd rather sleep later." (Sleep itself is an issue, which I discuss later in this chapter.)

- "I'm trying to lose weight."

- "I don't like breakfast food."

- "I'm just not hungry that early."

Skipping breakfast to get in a few more minutes of sleep is going to be harmful in the long run. A good protein breakfast provides the amino acids that allow a person to be more alert throughout the day. A few extra minutes of sleep won't have that effect.

Weight loss is often a big issue with middle school and high school students. But most studies suggest that skipping breakfast makes you hungrier later in the day, and more extreme hunger causes less scrutiny when it comes to choosing the more nutritious foods. Have you ever gone to the grocery store when you are hungry? Do you find that you begin to fill your cart with comfort foods and items that you might not normally purchase? Saving some calories in the morning is more likely to lead to more total calories for the day. In addition, the brain is suffering without its fuel. Learning, motivation, and attention are all at risk when students are hungry. The survival brain takes over and focuses only on the body's basic needs.

Obesity in adults and children has been linked to skipping breakfast as well, and obesity is harmful to the whole body, including the brain. Whenever the body is taxed by carrying excess weight, the heart and lungs have more work, which makes it more difficult to get much-needed nutrients and oxygen to the brain, possibly affecting learning.

Low levels of nutrition in school children are not just a socioeconomic issue. There are children from poverty who do not receive adequate nutrition, but there are also children of affluence who lack proper nutrition. Empty calories may fill tummies but not brains. It is not only that children are eating, but what they are eating that matters. Undernutrition can affect how often children are ill and absent from school, as well as the length of time it takes for recovery.

A longitudinal study by researcher Edward Frongillo at Cornell University confirms that nutrition affects reading. This study looked at twenty-one thousand students and found some gender differences. For instance, girls had more difficulty with reading when nutritious food was unavailable to them or in short supply. Their social skills were also affected (Jyoti, Frongillo, & Jones, 2005). This study builds on previous work by Alaimo, Olson, and Frongillo (2002), which found that hunger and poverty in the United States are severe enough to extensively impair the educational and psychosocial development of school-age children and adolescents.

The Learning Brain's Diet

What should our children be eating in order to maximize their brain power? Since every household is different and everyone has different tastes, the following sections just offer some suggestions as to the types of foods for each meal.

Breakfast

Many people who engage in brain research believe that for the brain to function optimally, it must start the day with protein. Remember that protein creates tyrosine, which helps neurons manufacture norepinephrine and dopamine. These two neurotransmitters help keep the brain alert and awake, and they help make connections for learning as well as focus the brain.

A protein breakfast can consist of some of the following: eggs, meats, poultry, cheese, fruit, yogurt, and complex carbohydrates. A breakfast menu might be the following:

- Vegetable omelet

- Apple or orange slices

- Multigrain bread with butter

or

- Yogurt

- Granola or whole-grained cereal

or

- Whole-grain waffle

- Walnuts

- Cheese cubes

Some kids may prefer breakfast pizza with such items as sausage, potatoes, eggs, and cheese made on whole-wheat crust, or even cold pizza.

Lunch and Snacks

Experts also suggest that protein be served for lunch. The brain needs to remain alert throughout the day, so dopamine and norepinephrine must continue to be manufactured. Here are some brain-nourishing lunch dishes:

- Peanut or almond butter on multigrain bread

- Walnuts or almonds (for schools that don't allow nuts or nut butters, Sunbutter, a peanut-free alternative made with sunflower seeds, is a good solution)

- Strawberries or blueberries

or

- Turkey breast on whole-wheat bread

- Cherry tomatoes

- Yogurt

or

- Left-over pizza

- Carrot sticks

- A banana

Many students become cranky and even tired without periodic nutrition and require snacks. However, it is not always possible for the schools to allow a snack time for them. Graham crackers and dried fruits are an option for students who need something if you are willing to allow this in your class from time to time.

Dinner

Dinner may be the time to add carbohydrates to create tryptophan. This produces serotonin in the brain and is calming.

A dinner menu might be:

- Mashed potatoes, sweet potatoes, or yams

- Grilled chicken, lean beef, or grilled fish

- Fresh vegetables, grilled vegetables, or salad

- Fresh fruit, fruit smoothie, or applesauce

- Whole-grain rolls

To Sleep; Perchance to Remember

The importance of sleep for learning cannot be overemphasized. The amount of sleep a child gets each night affects the amount of information that can be stored in long-term memory. It is true that a child can appear to learn something one day and forget it the next, but without proper sleep, there is little chance of remembering. In order to turn short-term memories into long-term memories, sleep is required.

Sleep also:

- Gives the body energy

- Helps with brain development

- Helps consolidate memories

- Helps reduce stress

- Aids in focus, attention, and concentration

Nevertheless, according to Gary Small (2002), about 100 million Americans do not get enough sleep.

We would all like to have children enter their classrooms each day having had the proper amount of sleep. If this were to occur on a regular basis, student brains would be much more receptive to learning and remembering.

The need for sleep depends on various factors, including age. Infants usually require about sixteen to eighteen hours of sleep per day, early childhood estimates are between ten and twelve hours per day, and middle schoolers and teenagers need about nine hours per day on average. Most adults need about seven or eight hours of sleep per day.

The Stages of Sleep

Nighttime sleep usually has five stages: stages 1, 2, 3, 4, and then rapid eye movement (REM) sleep. Let's follow eleven-year-old Brennan through the stages of sleep. Brennan gets ready for bed, lies down, and begins to relax as he thinks about the day's events or perhaps what is on the agenda for tomorrow. If he is stressed about upcoming events or embarrassed about previous ones, his body and brain may take longer to relax. Eventually, though, his breathing will become more regular and his muscles will loosen.

Stage 1   Brennan first falls into stage 1, a light sleep from which he can easily be awakened. During this stage, he may have small, uncontrolled muscle movements that awaken him, and he may have visual images that seem almost hallucinatory if he were awakened. His eyes move slowly back and forth during this stage, his heart rate steadies, and his blood pressure goes down. When Brennan was awake, the electrical activity in his brain produced beta waves. (See table 3.1 for information on brain waves.) Beta waves, which get us through our days and help us get things done, cycle in the brain between twelve and forty times per second. (Cycling is the term used to explain the strength of the activity in the brain, that is, the way the neurons are connecting.) Now Brennan goes into a calmer wave pattern called alpha, a state of relaxed alertness.

Table 3.1 Types of Brain Waves

Beta	This is the brain wave of the conscious mind. The brain is cycling twelve to forty times per second. It is in this state that we accomplish our everyday activities.
Alpha	This is the brain wave that signifies relaxed alertness. The brain is cycling eight to twelve times per second.
Theta	This is the brain wave that occurs just as we drift off to sleep and as we awaken. It is found in both stages 1 and 2. The brain in this state is cycling four to seven times per second.
Delta	This is the brain wave that occurs during deep sleep. The brain is cycling one to three times per second.

Quickly, he will enter the next type of wave, theta. In the theta wave state, Brennan is in the first stage of sleep.

Stage 2 After five to ten minutes or so, Brennan's brain enters stage 2 sleep, when brain waves change. Theta waves now cause the spindles and spikes (seen in an electroencephalogram, which measures brain waves) that are evidence that the brain is indeed in stage 2. Brennan's eye movements of stage 1 cease, and he sleeps more deeply. Although he is still easily awakened, he is more likely to realize that he was asleep than he was in stage 1. Larger brain waves are seen in stage 2, and bodily functions slow down.

Stage 3 After another ten minutes or so, Brennan enters stage 3 sleep, the beginning of deep sleep and characterized by delta waves. Dr. William Dement, author of *The Promise of Sleep* (1999), describes stage 3 as the time that the spindles and spikes of stage 2 are swallowed up by the delta waves. It is this process that will put Brennan into stage 4.

Stage 4 If Brennan were awakened from this deep sleep stage, he would feel groggy, and it would take him some time to function normally. Brennan's muscles are completely relaxed now, and his breathing is slow and regular, as is his heart rate. During stage 4, Brennan's young body will release growth hormone, which will help his body grow and repair damaged cells (Dement, 1999). His immune system will also be strengthened now.

Brennan will remain in stage 4 longer than his parents would. After about forty-five minutes in this stage, Brennan will move into a lighter stage of sleep. He is back to stage 3 and possibly stage 2 for just a few minutes before he goes to the final sleep stage, REM sleep.

REM Sleep   After about ninety minutes in the first stages of sleep, Brennan will enter the REM stage. His eyes will move back and forth behind his eyelids quite rapidly. In addition, Brennan's muscles will appear to be paralyzed. This is to keep him from acting out the dreams he is about to have. The brain waves Brennan experiences are now a combination of alpha, beta, and theta waves. They actually resemble those seen during wakefulness, although Brennan is sound asleep. This is just the first sleep cycle of the night, so Brennan's REM sleep lasts about ten minutes. He will then go back down through the other sleep stages, from stage 4 back to stage 1, and then back up, from stage 1 to stage 4, before he enters another REM stage.

As the night goes on, Brennan will experience five or six of these sleep cycles, and the length of his REM sleep will increase with each cycle. By his final cycle, Brennan's REM period will be up to about sixty minutes. During the early morning hours, the stress hormone cortisol will be released. This is not because he is stressed; rather, cortisol functions to get his energy sources ready for the day ahead. If Brennan awakens in the morning directly out of a REM period, he may remember one of his dreams.

Sleep and Memory

Although it has been known for many years that memories are "practiced" and consolidated during REM sleep, more research is

How Sleep Enhances Memory

What exactly happens during sleep to enhance memory? Matthew Walker (2009) of the University of California, Berkeley explains that during sleep, the brain transfers what it learned that day to storage systems for long-term memory. Different memories can be manipulated during various sleep stages. Initial studies were done on animals such as rats. The rat brains were exposed so electrodes could be placed on them. Then the rats were "taught" something, like learning to run a maze and find cheese at the end. As the rats were trained, the electrodes showed activity during different phases of the learning. All of these were recorded. This learning would include activity when the rat could not find the cheese as well as the activity that was created on finding the prize.

When the rats slept, they were monitored, and researchers could see identical patterns of activity during various sleep stages as they recorded during the learning experience. When the rats awoke, they were better at finding the cheese since their brains had "practiced" learning during sleep.

With humans, testing is a bit different since brains cannot be exposed. Instead, participants are taught information such as lists and then are allowed to sleep. Various people are awakened at different times in the sleep cycle and are tested on the material. The researchers discovered information, for example, that when we study a new language, the brain deals with auditory memories of the new phonemes it has heard, a new vocabulary and definitions, and even physical skills to pronounce the words correctly. The vocabulary is synthesized by the structure in the brain that handles factual information, the hippocampus, during stages 3 and 4. The motor skills of enunciation are processed during stage 2 non-REM sleep, but the auditory memories appear to be consolidated during all stages. Our emotional memories are encoded during REM sleep.

being done to discover what occurs during those first four stages of sleep, which are often called "non-REM." Robert Stickgold performed many sleep experiments in which he and his colleagues concluded that graduate students who slept less than the desired eight hours of sleep remembered less than those who slept the full amount (Stickgold, Whidbee, Schirmer, Patel, & Hobson, 2000). It seems that the lack of the final REM stage or stages of sleep accounted for the lack of memory. New learning is practiced during sleep, and the connections that are made between neurons when the learning first occurred reconnect at night when we sleep (Blakeslee, 2000).

The act of cramming for a test is something most of us have done. Cramming, however, shortens the amount of sleep that we get and encourages a working memory experience rather than a long-term memory experience. Students should be encouraged to study a little each night right before bedtime. While they sleep, their brains will practice the material they just covered, and little by little all of the material will be stored in long-term memory. Those who cram forget the information after the test, have wasted a lot of their time, and have lost sleep that is so important for a healthy brain and body.

Making the Right Moves

Ken Wesson (2005) says that the ability to skip indicates reading readiness, and many reading specialists agree. The research linking movement and learning is piling up, and educators should take a close look at it. Movement and exercise make a difference in many academic abilities.

Let's consider the three basic premises of what exercise does for the brain:

1. Exercise increases heart rate and respiration. Therefore, more blood and oxygen go to the brain in a shorter amount of

time and in larger quantities. This also increases the number of blood vessels that go to the brain and help it receive larger amounts of oxygen and nutrients (Hannaford, 2005).

2.   Exercise causes the brain to release brain-derived neurotropic factor, which is essentially food to help the brain grow (Medina, 2008; Ratey, 2008).

3.   Exercise affects the dentate gyrus by increasing blood flow to this specific area. This is part of the hippocampus that aids memory (Medina, 2008; Ratey, 2008).

There's more, too. According to many researchers, learning doesn't take place without movement. Consider the fact that movement helps to build the vestibular system, which helps with balance. Along with that system, movement requires the cerebellum. Because the cerebellum helps the body navigate its way in space, it grows many connections that later are used to help guide that brain through many thought processes. This shows us how interrelated movement and learning actually are (Hannaford, 2005).

John Ratey, author of *Spark: The New Revolutionary Science of Exercise and the Brain,* has worked on studies all over the country to see how exercise affects learning. He explains that aerobic exercise, any kind of extended activity that makes individuals breathe hard as they use large muscle groups at an even and regular pace, "wakes up" the prefrontal cortex of the brain where impulse control takes place. Students with many learning and behavioral problems have responded positively to beginning the day or a class period doing such exercise. They are then able to focus and concentrate on their studies.

The key to these changes is sustained aerobic exercise, not just movement. Positive results were found in an eighth-grade class taught by Allison Cameron (2012). Her students began a program of raising their heart rates between 65 and 75 percent for twenty minutes, and she tested them before and after the exercise. She found that they went up one year in reading and one year in math between February and the end of the school year.

Ward Elementary School in Winston-Salem, North Carolina, also worked on the brain-body connection with the Read and Ride program. Students spend time daily riding stationary bicycles and at the same time reading material they enjoy. As a result of this combination of adding movement to reading, their brains are growing, and the reading test scores show improvement (Underwood, 2009). Idaho teachers have started a Read and Ride program and found that students' behavior is also improving as a product of the exercise (Bodnar, 2011).

Sunshine Came Softly Through My Window

Sunlight is known to affect the way people feel. For several years, I taught in rooms with no windows. It was difficult for both the students and me, and at the time, I didn't know how detrimental it was. I found myself finding other areas with windows to do many lessons and activities. I told the students we were going on a "road trip" and sometimes even had class in the front hallway of the building where there was plenty of sunlight.

Studies by Kuller and Lindsten (1992) and the Heschong Mahone Group (1999), demonstrate a positive correlation between daylight and academic performance. Students spend a lot of time indoors as they sit at their computers and play with their digital toys, so it's important to give them opportunities to experience daylight at home and at school.

Parents need to be aware of the importance of daylight and natural lighting at home. When students do homework, they should be in an area with windows. If it is possible for them to work before the sun goes down, that is particularly advantageous. Some students have many after-school activities that makes this difficult, so be sure they are working using incandescent or full-spectrum lights.

Many schools are beginning to use full-spectrum lighting, but most still have fluorescent lights that often flicker, blink, and buzz and can disturb students. Instead, they should use the natural lighting as much as possible. They can also use incandescent lighting to enhance the natural daylight and perhaps bring in floor or table lamps for study or reading areas. In addition, they can put colored paper, preferably pink, over their fluorescent light covers to reduce the flickering.

Temperature, too, can affect the learning environment. A room that is kept between 68 and 72 degrees is ideal. Research suggests that a temperature of 74 degrees or higher may affect reading comprehension, and the ability to do math may be hindered if the temperature is 77 degrees or above (Jensen, 2005).

Brain-Body Basics

We know from Abraham Maslow (Maslow & Lowery, 1998) that there are basic needs that must be met for learning to take place. Physiological needs (e.g., food, clothing, shelter, air, and the need to urinate and defecate) come first. Students whose needs are not met will be in survival mode, which will initiate the stress response. The result will be that the brain will focus only on these physical survival needs. It is necessary for all schools to have at least the basic provisions for students to meet these needs:

- Water available, either with water bottles or a cooler and cups

- Healthy snacks for students who come to school without having eaten breakfast or those who have lunch early in the day

- Bathroom passes available at any time of the day

- A ventilation system that is working

Safety and Security

In order for students to learn, they must feel safe. This is second on Maslow's hierarchy of needs. In school, this means that students should feel free from threat from adults and fellow students:

- They should be aware that the school has a safety plan and be familiar with it.

- They should know and understand all classroom rules.

- They should know that teachers and administrators care about their physical safety.

Social Needs

Every brain has a need to belong. Recent research supports that learning is emotional and often based on relationships. This means teachers should not be "friends" to their students, but the more students like and respect their teachers, the more psychologically safe they will feel at school. This will also be motivating because students will want to please teachers they like. Here are some guidelines:

- Classrooms should offer a feeling of community.

- Students should spend time learning in groups and have the opportunity to truly get to know each other.

- At other times, students should be given choices as to how they want to learn: alone, in pairs, or in groups.

- Students can be given tasks to do in the classroom, which will help them feel that they are needed and are a part of the classroom community.

Cliques

Children of any age can get involved in specific groups or cliques. The social hierarchy can be seen in the classroom, the school, and the community, and it can affect not only social dynamics but also learning in the classroom. A study of middle school students revealed four social groups that students fall into (Giannetti & Sagarese, 2001), and most teachers agree that these groups exist at almost every grade level:

- *The popular group.* The in-group consists of students who fall into valued categories according to the student population. Sometimes the value is measured in terms of the culture of the school or area. Generally the "populars" are athletes, good looking, affluent, or smart. Any combination of these attributes seems to place students in the popular group. About 35 percent of the middle school population fall into this category. What is interesting is that these students appear to be poised and confident, but when they were interviewed, the researchers discovered that most were worried that their popularity would soon end.

- *The fringe group.* These students live at the edge of the popular group. They want to be popular, and sometimes they are included in popular activities and sometimes not. The result is that this approximately 10 percent of the population is stressed because they never quite know where they belong.

- *The loners.* About 10 percent of the population are kids who don't hang out with anyone. They act as if they want to be alone, although most of them revealed that they really didn't want it that way. Some of these students are alone because they don't get along with the other students. They may be poor or not bathe or wash their clothes. A loner may also be a student who is very bright and has trouble relating to classmates or they to him or her. Many of these students are angry about their social status.

- *The friendship circles.* These students have three or four friends they feel safe with. They support each other and have no desire to be popular, but some of them may show some hostility toward the popular group. About 45 percent of students fall into this category. The friendship circles are made up of different groups of students. Some may be labeled geeks, nerds, wild, or gangs. They appear to be satisfied and happy at school.

You can see how the majority of students are stressed by their social situation. It may be great to be popular, but if they have to worry about whether their popularity will last, that can cause great concern. Let's take a look at exactly what stress is and what it does to the brain and the body.

Stress Can Hurt the Body and the Brain

Since there is good stress as well as bad stress, it is necessary to understand the effects of each. Good stress is the mild stress that we feel when we do such things as go on an interview or a blind date. This stress actually causes the brain to release some adrenaline and other chemicals that may help us respond in these situations.

A short bout of stress is sometimes called "tolerable" stress: the brain and body recover quickly from it. However, chronic stress on both the body and the brain can cause great harm to anyone, young or old. It can:

- Affect learning by physically changing the brain

- Affect learning by temporarily blocking the transmission of messages in the brain

- Affect learning by lowering the immune system and putting health in jeopardy

- Affect the cardiovascular system by blocking arteries
- Affect sleep
- Affect reproduction
- Cause anxiety, depression, and other psychiatric disorders

It is necessary to understand the stress response in order to help prevent it as well as to be able to relate to children who are suffering the consequences from chronic stress. It's also important to know that stress in pregnant women affects the way their babies' brains respond to stress. The stress chemicals affect the limbic area of the brain first, so both the structures for memory and emotional regulation can be affected. Therefore, Mom's stress can cause both emotional and cognitive problems. Second, the baby's stress response system becomes overloaded with chemicals such as cortisol, and the brain has difficulty controlling it. Consequently, these children may go through life with poor stress control (Medina, 2008).

Following the Stress Response

Our stress response comes from the days when we were in danger of physical harm. (Lions and tigers and bears. Oh my!) Therefore, during the stress response, your brain decides whether a situation is threatening to you. Under threatening conditions, the brain feels there are two choices: get away from the threat or fight the threat. Hence, it is called the fight-or-flight response. Today, however, our stressors are much different from those of old. Now we are more likely to initiate the stress response from very different threats, like public speaking, having a root canal, facing a difficult class, or being late for an important appointment. Regardless, the stress response behaves in our bodies and brains in the same way as it did in the past.

When a threatening situation presents itself, it is necessary to harness the energy in your body to run or fight. This is begun through a process of chemical release in the brain. The reticular activating system, the first brain filter, realizes that something is different and sends out neurotransmitters throughout the brain. The second brain filter, the amygdala, receives the chemical messages quickly and releases a hormone to alert the hypothalamus. This structure sends a message to the pituitary gland, located close by in the brain. The pituitary releases a stress chemical to alert the adrenal glands, located above the kidneys. You can see how quickly the brain-body connection occurs. The adrenals release cortisol and adrenaline. This chain of events is called the HPA axis (the hypothalamic-pituitary-adrenal axis). These chemicals cause more oxygen to go to the lungs and more blood flow to go to your extremities—your arms (in case you are going to fight) and your legs (in case you are going to run). When it's working well, this axis allows us to handle stress and return to a normal brain-body state afterward.

The brain quickly prioritizes the important bodily functions. Reproduction, digestion, and growth can be put on hold. Even the immune system changes as it revs up for injuries rather than fighting the cold you currently have. The blood that is being used to digest your lunch is sent to help you fight or flee; after all, why digest lunch if you might be lunch!

The HPA axis requires balance. If it becomes unbalanced due to too much cortisol or adrenaline that results from chronic stress or too many bouts of acute stress, the situation gets out of control. The result can be heart disease, a compromised immune system, and inadequate memory formation (McEwen, 2002).

Recognizing chronically stressed kids can be a challenge. If their immune systems are compromised, they may be sick often and absent from school. Unfortunately, being absent, missing class work, and having to explain the situation can cause more stress, setting up a vicious cycle.

Nevertheless, we can help stressed kids in several ways—for example:

- Make sure they have strong relationships: a support team, group, or community.

- Make sure they get enough exercise.

- Make sure they are getting enough sleep.

- Provide them with a nonthreatening environment.

- Try having them listen to soothing music.

The consequences of chronic stress are dangerous. Not only can it interfere with learning and memory, but it also can cause serious mental and physical health problems.

What Does Bullying Do to the Brain?

Physical and emotional abuse of children can interrupt and change the developing brain. Being bullied can be chronically stressful and cause cognitive as well as psychological problems. Some studies revealed some disturbing results; for example, children who are picked on may have brains that are similar to those of children who have been physically or sexually abused.

When brain development is interrupted by stressful situations like bullying, one of the results may be the lack of or slowing down of neurogenesis, the growth of new neurons. The neurogenesis process is also part of learning new things. When the brain is motivated to learn something new, new neurons are recruited to be part of the neural network that forms the memory of that learning. Bullied students may have great difficulty in learning new things.

Chronic stress from bullying may keep these students in the stress response. With the constant release of stress hormones, the brain can have great difficulty in focusing attention on learning.

It may not take much time for the brain changes to take effect. Dr. Martin Teicher (2002) discovered that the corpus callosums of some young adults who were bullied had developed differently from those of young adults who had not experienced abuse. The corpus callosum connects the two hemispheres of the brain and is necessary for visual processing and memory. He found that there was less of a myelin coating on these neurons, and we know that myelin assists with quick transmission of messages.

At the University of Ottawa, studies found that twelve-year-olds who had been verbally abused by peers had abnormal levels of the stress hormone cortisol. Girls who were bullied had less of the hormone than other girls, and the bullied boys had more cortisol than boys who had not been bullied. The theory is that the bullied girls learned to control their responses to the bullying and their brains released less cortisol as a result. This defense mechanism puts less stress on the body. These variances can affect the immune system as well as memory (Vaillancourt, 2004).

Summary

This chapter has examined many of the effects of experience and environment on the brain and the body. It is necessary to understand the whole child in order to teach the most important skill of their academic careers: reading.

Encouraging appropriate sleep and nutrition and explaining why they are so important to children can affect the ease with which learning can take place. Exercise is also necessary for brain and body development and therefore for learning. Parents and schools should ensure that children are encouraged to exercise and provided sufficient time to exercise, and teachers need to be aware of the importance of movement in the classroom.

The effects of social interactions and stress should not be understated. The social strata at schools affect all students. Social hierarchies can affect the stress levels of students, and we know that stress can interfere with learning. Students may be stressed due to experiences at home, on the bus, on the playground, or in class. Parents and educators should understand the stress response and recognize some of the consequences of stress.

Everything children eat, how they sleep, how much exercise they have, and how they feel about the classroom and social experience will affect how well they learn to read.

CHAPTER 4

Breaking the Code

As emmie's teacher was emphasizing the sounds in the word *dog*, an interesting conversation ensued:

Miss Katherine:	Children, listen to the word *dog*. /D/o/g/ has three sounds. Can you make those sounds?
Emmie (interrupting):	My gramma's dog has three sounds: woof, woof, woof!

The adventure begins. The brain must learn to listen for the sounds in words and recognize them. Reading is a complex cognitive process that has five essential components built on brain development and experience. As you read the words on this page, your brain has several systems it calls on simultaneously to do the tasks that comprise the simple act of reading—simple, that is, if you are not a struggling reader.

Those five components of reading are phonemic awareness, phonics, vocabulary, fluency, and reading comprehension. Often people use *phonics* and *phonemic awareness* interchangeably, but there is an important distinction: phonemic awareness relates exclusively to sounds, while phonics is the connection between sounds and letters. Table 4.1 describes the differences.

Reading specialists and researchers are constantly looking for predictors of reading success. What does a child need to know and be able to do in order to be a good reader? Many students with reading disabilities have poor phonemic awareness skills (Stanovich, 1998).

Table 4.1 Phonemic Awareness Versus Phonics

Phonemic Awareness: An Auditory Skill	Phonics: A Visual Skill
Ability to recognize the individual sounds of spoken language and how they can be blended together, segmented, and manipulated	An instructional approach that links the sounds of spoken language to printed letters Graphemes:
• Involve sound • Tasks can be done with the eyes closed	• Involve sound and print • Tasks involve looking at print
Examples:	Examples:
• Say the word *dog*. Ask students to say each sound they hear in the word: /d/ /o/g/. • Ask students to listen to each sound in a word and say the word. This focuses on the sounds of spoken language and how they can be blended, segmented, and manipulated. It also provides the basis for understanding the alphabetic principle and lays the foundation for phonics and spelling	• Write the word. Ask students to say each sound in the word and blend the sounds together to read the word: /dog/. • Ask students to listen to each sound in a word and spell the word using letter tiles. • Show how the sounds of spoken language are represented by letters and spellings.

There are two theories of reading and letter naming. Most research supports that knowing the letter names is an early predictor of good reading (Bond & Dykstra, 1967; McBride-Chang, 1999). Others believe that since the letters of the alphabet do not sound like their names, knowing the alphabet is confusing when it comes time to learn phonemic awareness (Lindamood, 1995). Many children learn the alphabet song long before they enter school, but whether they associate the letter name with the letter representation is another matter.

Maeve gobbles up books. Literally. Every book she can get her hands on goes directly into her mouth. This is a baby's first approach to interacting with a book. It's an important step that signals curiosity and a desire to know more about the object. When

Maeve's mother reads to her and Maeve notices the print on the page (which may be accentuated by Mom's finger gliding beneath the words), she begins to discover that print has meaning. The next goal is for Maeve to learn how to handle a book properly by holding the right side up and turning one page at a time. At age three or four, Maeve will begin to notice letters in her name. This is all part of becoming really familiar with print.

We hope that when Maeve is a preschooler, she will understand more about text. For instance, she will know that text is read from left to right and from the top of the page to the bottom if reading has been modeled for her enough times for her brain to store the procedure. She may know the letters of the entire alphabet by now or will begin to learn them. It is important that she realize that the words she hears are made up of sounds.

Much of the understanding children bring with them to preschool depends on their experiences and interest. Consider two little girls, Rose and Lily.

By the age of two, Rose recognized every letter of the alphabet. The magnetic letters were on the refrigerator. If Rose's mom asked her to go find the R, Rose would disappear into the kitchen and return in less than a minute proudly holding the R in her hand. This was a game that Rose enjoyed. There were no flash cards, and the moment Rose was tired of the game, it ended.

Rose learned that each letter made a sound. Besides learning this from her mom and other caregivers (they would make the sound when Rose brought a letter to them), she was also exposed after the age of two to videos that taught her letter sounds (*The Letter Factory* by Leap Frog) and toys that played the sounds (the Leap Frog Bus). Many children do not have access to these extras, but of course there are many other ways to learn the letters and the sounds they make.

Many children this young do not show an interest in knowing the letters and their sounds yet, and that is perfectly okay. For instance, Rose's playmate, Lily, could sing the alphabet song by the age of two, but she had little or no interest in learning letter names or sounds. No matter what letter Lily's mom asked for, Lily brought back random letters and announced that each was the letter B.

Children who enter kindergarten knowing the letters and sounds will have an easier time with the curriculum. Many kindergarten teachers prefer students to be able to recognize the letters and count to 10. Rose may have an advantage over Lily if Lily does not develop an interest before she enters preschool or kindergarten. But that doesn't mean that Lily won't be able to catch up.

Phonemic Awareness

Phonemic awareness is the ability to hear and manipulate sounds in spoken language. Children who understand that words are made up of individual letters, each of which makes a sound that is represented by a letter, are on their way to reading.

According to reading researcher Sally Shaywitz (2003), readers need to be able to do the following five tasks:

1. Hear the beginning sounds of words and recognize when words begin with the same sounds.

2. Separate the initial sound of a word.

3. Separate the final sounds in a word.

4. Combine sounds as in blending.

5. Break words into their separate sounds.

The greatest indication that a child will be a successful reader is his or her phonemic awareness combined with knowledge of the individual letters (Bond & Dykstra, 1967). Middle and high school students who lack this ability (and there are many) can be taught these skills. The absence of phonemic awareness is the greatest problem of struggling readers.

Assessing and Teaching Phonemic Awareness

"I can make a rhyme every time!" This was the mantra in my pre-K/kindergarten class when I began teaching. It was a fun game for children who knew their sounds and letters but a frustration for those who did not. The children often offered words that had similar meanings but not the same sounds. And some would shout out a word that started with the same sound but did not rhyme with the word.

From teaching kindergarten, I jumped to a seventh-grade position. To kill some time at the end of one class period in my language arts class, I decided to play the game. Seventh graders are not very different from kindergartners when it comes to loving games and talking. But I was shocked to discover that so many of my students had trouble with rhyming. The good readers were excellent at the game, but some of my struggling students shied away from participating. This was before I even knew about phonemic awareness. But I did know how important it was that students be able to listen, pay attention, and remember bits of information. And at the middle school level, those were my objectives in playing the rhyming game. (Did you know that there are over one thousand words that rhyme with the word *nation*? That was always a good word to start the game with these adolescents.)

Marilyn Jaeger Adams (1990), one of the foremost experts on learning to read, explains phonemic awareness well. From birth, we encourage babies to listen to and express sounds that they hear in their environment. But what we are encouraging is not really the sounds, but the meaning of those sounds. As babies grow, we are thrilled when they have names for the objects they desire. Parents encourage their children to put meaning to their surroundings. However, when it is time to learn to read or acquire prereading skills, these children are now asked to focus not on the meaning of words but their individual sounds. When it is first spoken, "M-o-m-m-y" is a person whose attention is needed, not a word broken down into individual sounds. The words must be unpacked, so to speak.

It is known that the brain cannot attend to more than one thing at a time. As these young brains hear words, the brain automatically goes to the meaning of the word and what behavior should follow the understanding of the word or words spoken. The brain then has to be retrained—actually rewired—to listen not for meaning but for sound. In other words, the brain must learn to attend to that which it has learned not to attend to. No wonder learning to read is so difficult!

If I ask you to listen only to the initial phoneme in a word and not to attend to the meaning of the word, can you do so easily? You will find yourself, like most other good readers who find facility with our language, zipping from the definition or the visual you have stored in your memory back to the initial sound. When you read the word *elephant,* you quickly picture the gray-skinned animal with a huge trunk and then separate that first sound and say "eh." Try it with a few words, and see if you agree. Then imagine what a new reader must go through to play this new game. And because once we have children taking the words apart and putting them back together, we want them to go back to the comprehension.

Adams (1990) suggests that phonemic awareness goes through a series of stages:

1. *Rhyming:* The ability to hear rhyming sounds as in nursery rhymes. Nursery rhymes are an easy way to begin to teach phonemic awareness. Since my granddaughter loves the Disney princesses, I taught her the jump-rope rhyme I learned as a child: *Cinderella dressed in yellow (yella) went upstairs to kiss her fella.* From there, four-year-old Emmie began to

substitute words—for instance, "Cinderella dressed in red went upstairs to make her bed!" "Cinderella dressed in blue went upstairs to tie her shoe."

2. *Oddity tasks:* Determining whether sounds are the same or different. *Example:* "Which word does not rhyme? Cat, pig, hat."

3. *Blending and syllable splitting:* Giving children the individual phonemes of a word and asking them to put the sounds together; asking what the first sound is in a word and asking them what is left. *Examples:* "Listen to these word parts. D-o-g. Can you put the word together?" "Listen to the word *cat.* Can you tell me what the first sound of *cat* is? What sounds are left?"

4. *Phonemic segmentation:* Having students tap or clap each sound in a word. *Example:* "Listen to this word. *Hat.* Can you say *hat* sound by sound?"

5. *Phonemic manipulation:* Adding, deleting, or moving a phoneme to make a different word. *Example:* "Say the word *dog* without the /d/."

A report by the National Literacy Panel (2008) concluded that there is a progression when teaching phonemic awareness skills. It appears that the younger the child is, the more likely he is to begin understanding whole words such as *cup* + *cake* = *cupcake.* This blending of and deleting whole words makes sense to the children. The syllable level then comes next—that is, being able to divide a word by its syllables, such as *teach* + *er* = *teacher.* The phoneme level followed this as in *c* + *a* + *t* = *cat.*

It makes sense that the process of dividing up and putting together groups of sounds is easiest with words that are previously stored in memory. Thus, the whole-word approach is the simplest step. Taking words and dividing them into their syllables is a little harder because the brain must listen for the breaks in the sounds. Finally, taking those words apart sound by sound is a more complex task. It is comforting to know that we have these benchmarks to follow as we teach phonemic awareness.

The ABCs of the ABCs

Knowing the letter names and their sounds is the first step to becoming a good reader. The ability to hear and recognize individual phonemes is crucial to reading success for most students. The "aha" moment in reading is when a child realizes that the words he hears are made up of smaller parts—individual sounds that each letter represents. The research suggests that children who can attain phonemic awareness before entering school are likely to succeed in reading (Shaywitz, 2003).

I cannot stress enough that phonemic awareness involves sounds. Visual representations are not necessary for this reading readiness skill. It's not what the students see; it's what they hear. Phonemic awareness:

- Focuses on the sounds of spoken language and how they can be blended, segmented, and manipulated.

- Provides the basis for understanding the alphabetic principle and lays the foundation for phonics and spelling.

Mirror, Mirror

In chapter 1, I discussed the incredible discovery of the mirror neuron system. In this chapter, we return to this system in relationship to children's learning about phonemes. Since the mirror neurons were discovered, researchers have been trying to make connections between this system and other forms of learning.

Because the connection between mirror neurons and emotions is so strong, children may be able to mirror the desire to read and understand what they and others are reading. Mary Ann Wolf (2008), director of the Center for Reading and Language Research at Tufts University, says that learning to read begins with the first book a child has read to him or her. Perhaps within the first few weeks after birth, the primary caregiver sits with the infant in his or her arms and reads a book in a loving manner. It could be any book. In this way, the baby is introduced to reading in the warmth of someone's arms who shows love and attention, meets primary needs, and reads in a soothing voice. If that reading continues in the same way throughout childhood, the child grows to love books and listening to others read, and eventually begins to recognize the sounds that are heard and then the letters that are seen.

Neurons That Fire Together

Thinking back to the two reading pathways from chapter 2, we can get an idea of how phonemic awareness works. When the parieto-temporal pathway is activated, it involves seeing the letters, sounding them out, and putting them together in such a way that they form a word that makes sense to the reader. Let's take the simple word *cat*. The reader sees each letter individually and says the sounds: c–a–t, c–a–t, cat. At this point the child sees the mental picture of the cat, but until those sounds come together to form that word, the child is using all of his or her working memory to sound out those letters. The picture of the cat is not yet in his or her head. Once the visuotemporal pathway is used due to repetitions of the word, immediate recognition takes place. In other words, the picture of the cat pops up as the child sees the word. Phonemic awareness allows this transfer to take place.

Dr. Seuss and Mother Goose?

Parents, preschool teachers, and primary teachers regularly ask me to identify appropriate books to read to a child. Let's start with the youngest children first. From birth through early childhood (age eight), most kids enjoy rhymes. Dr. Seuss and Mother Goose not only rhyme with each other, they also have fun and easy rhymes for children to hear. At this age, it is more beneficial for children to hear the sounds of the phonemes as they rhyme than to have a fabulous story. If there is a wonderful story involved that the child can understand, even better.

Some of the Mother Goose rhymes may not seem appropriate for all ages, but most of them are harmless, fun, and educational. Mother Goose creates some delightful rhyming stories out of a wide variety of sounds, blendings, and endings.

According to Mem Fox (2001), beloved children's author and reading expert, in order for a child to be able to read, he should hear a thousand books read to him. That may seem like a lot, but over the first five years of life, it is certainly attainable. In middle-class families, children are often read at least two books per day. In one year, that equals over seven hundred books, so it's not hard to get to one thousand in just a few years. Does it matter if the child wants to hear the same book over and over again? Definitely not. Repetition is good for the brain. Children get satisfaction from being able to predict what is going to happen, so they love hearing stories over and over. They become accustomed to the sounds in the words and eventually can "memorize" the book and read it back to you. And after enough repetition, they will also start to visually identify some of the words in their favorite story.

Jim Trelease, author of *The Read Aloud Handbook* (2004), has this to say about reading aloud to a child: "Whenever an adult reads to a child, three important things are happening simultaneously and painlessly: (1) a pleasure-connection is being made between child and book; (2) both parent and child are learning something from the book they're sharing (double learning); and (3) the adult is pouring sounds and syllables called words into the child's ear" (p. 4). He then goes on to say, "Inside the ear these words collect in a reservoir called the listening vocabulary. Eventually, if you pour enough words into it, the reservoir starts to overflow—pouring words into the speaking vocabulary, reading vocabulary, and writing vocabulary. And all have their origin in the listening vocabulary" (p. 33).

Those words should be shared with every parent, primary caregiver, and teacher. We can't do too much reading aloud to children. The extent of its benefits probably goes beyond what we know about the brain and reading. But the research agrees that children who are read to have an advantage over those who are not.

Getting to the Core

The foundational skills outlined by the Common Core State Standards Initiative, which was led by the Council of Chief State School Officers and the National Governors Association (2010), have been constructed by using the quality state standards as well as international models, educators from all grade levels, state departments of education, parents, students, and others too numerous to mention. By synthesizing the best elements of all work related to standards-based education, the Common Core groups developed these standards as a work in progress with the promise of revisions as new research with better evidence surfaces.

The goal of these standards is not to tell teachers how to teach but rather to define what students should know and be able to do— for example, "Demonstrate understanding of the organization and basic features of print," one of the standards for students from kindergarten to fifth grade. The language arts standards include not only requirements for English language arts, but also requirements for literacy in history and social studies, science, and technical subjects. In fact, every content area has its own literacy, and each of us must be responsible for setting the expectations for being able to read, understand, and communicate in a literate manner in all content areas. The core standards appear to follow the best practices in teaching reading skills suggested by Marilyn Adams (1990), Louisa Moats and Susan Hall (2005), and others.

Phonemic awareness standards are used only at the kindergarten and first-grade levels. Beyond that it is thought that students will not need them. By the second grade, children should have learned these skills:

At the Kindergarten Level

- Recognize and produce rhyming words.

- Count, pronounce, blend, and segment syllables in spoken words.

- Blend and segment onsets and rimes of single-syllable spoken words.

- Isolate and pronounce the initial, medial vowel, and final sounds (phonemes) in three-phoneme words.

- Add or substitute individual sounds (phonemes) in simple one-syllable words to make new words.

At Grade 1

- Distinguish long from short vowel sounds in spoken single-syllable words.

- Orally produce single-syllable words by blending sounds (phonemes), including consonant blends.

- Isolate and pronounce initial, medial vowel, and final sounds (phonemes) in spoken single-syllable words.

- Segment spoken single-syllable words.

- Segment spoken single-syllable words into their complete sequence of individual sounds (phonemes).

Teaching Phonemic Awareness

Phonemic awareness is the understanding that the sounds of spoken language are combined to form words. Phonics is the understanding that there is a relationship between letters and sounds through written language. In order for phonics instruction to be beneficial, children first must be aware of the sounds of their language. Once they can hear the phonemes and manipulate them, the task of assigning the sounds to a letter in written words becomes easier.

Activities

The activities that follow may be used by teachers and parents to assist children in learning the sounds of the letters. When phonemic awareness is a team effort, children learn more quickly and easily.

Name That Sound!

There have been many names for this game, which has several variations, many based on the work of Marilyn Adams (Adams, Foorman, Lundberg, & Beeler, 2004). In general, this is a fun way to improve listening skills and help students focus on sounds. Rather than beginning with the letters, it encourages students to identify some of the commonly heard yet somewhat distinctive sounds that they hear every day.

Perhaps there are sounds that are distinctive in your home or classroom: the school bell or the doorbell, the sound of the heating and cooling system turning off and on, the slight buzz of the fluorescent bulbs in the classroom, the hum of the refrigerator at home, and the sound of a door closing. Begin by making a list of common sounds that you can duplicate or record—for example:

Sneezing	Clapping
Coughing	Finger snapping
Sniffling	Foot stomping
Drawers opening	Throat clearing
Notes on the piano	Hammering
Computer turning on	Beating a drum
Blowing a whistle	

Begin the game by asking the children to close and cover their eyes and listen for the sound. (This can be done with a single child, too.) In a classroom, determine whether you want students to call out the sound in unison or if you want them to wait to be called on. In either case, be sure to keep track of the students who are having difficulty identifying the sounds.

Once the children have become accustomed to the game and can identify one sound easily, it is time to add another sound and ask them to identify the sounds in order. You can then add a third sound. After identifying a series of sounds, a variation of this game is giving them the same series of sounds, but eliminating one sound to see if they can identify which one is missing.

Some older struggling readers may have missed out on phonemic awareness instruction or have some issues that make it difficult to hear and identify sounds. It's never too late to help them out. Some middle and even high school students can have fun with this game as you add more distinctive or humorous sounds. Sound effects are available on CDs and downloadable from various Web sites (e.g., http://www.grsites.com/archive/sounds and http://www.soundsnap.com/). Toilets flushing, burping, the backfiring of a car, animal sounds, and any sounds associated with technology are distinctive and can be amusing, too.

Listening for sounds helps students focus on their listening abilities. From games like this one, you can move into letter sounds, the sounds of speech.

Say What?

This activity involves reading something very familiar to children (or a single child) and replacing a word or words in it with other words. Children listen and identify what word actually belongs in the sentence or phrase. Nursery rhymes, poetry, sayings, and normal phrases often heard may be used—for example:

- Mary, Mary, quite contrary, how does your hair grow?

- Little Boy Blue, come blow your nose.

- I do not like blue eggs and ham.

- Way to stop!

- Look no ways before crossing.

For older students, lyrics to popular songs, poetry, expressions, and even content can be used:

- Do you ever feel like a house of sticks? (Katy Perry lyrics)

- It is the east, and Juliet is the moon.

- I'm dreaming of a green Christmas.

- In fourteen hundred ninety-two, Magellan sailed the ocean blue.

Rhyming Pictures

This popular game can be found online (e.g., on the Scholastic Web site: http://teacher.scholastic.com/activities/bll/reggie/home/index.htm). It involves showing children four pictures of common objects or animals. One child says the names of the pictures aloud and then announces which two rhyme. An example is shown in figure 4.1.

❖ FIGURE 4.1: *Find the Rhyming Words*

What Do You Say?

For this activity, begin by saying, "I say *ball*. Billy, what do you say?" Billy will respond with, "I say hall [or another word that rhymes with *ball*]." Then Billy says, "I say *hat*. Ari, what do you say?" The game continues in this way. If the next person cannot come up with a rhyme, he or she may pass to the next person: "Sally, what do you say?" Be certain that everyone understands that there is no shame in not knowing a rhyming word. What is important is that the children listen carefully to the rhymes and be sure that the responding child does indeed offer a word that rhymes with the previous word.

A variation of this game in the classroom is for the teacher to begin and the entire class to respond with rhyming words by raising hands and waiting to be called on. With older students, this can make the game even more fun as they compete for the most rhymes or the most obscure words. Even a nonsense word supplies the teacher with the knowledge that the student can hear the sounds and make rhymes.

Every Sound Is Worth a Clap or a Tap

In this activity, children tap out the individual sounds in words. You demonstrate the activity by saying a word like *dog* and then tapping out the individual sounds with a pencil or other object: "D-tap-O-tap-G." After the demonstration, the child or children join in the activity along with the you.

Syllable Segmenting

Another important component of phonemic awareness is the ability to hear the syllables in words. Clapping or tapping can be used to divide words into their syllables as well as for sounds. The activity begins with you demonstrating how a word, such as *kitchen*, is divided into two syllables. As the children master two-syllable words, continue on to words with more syllables.

Sound Substitution

An even more sophisticated skill is the ability to hear a sound, remove it, and replace it with another sound. Since children love to sing, using sound substitutions through familiar songs works well for most teachers. In the song "I've Been Working on the Railroad," the refrain of, "Fie, fi, fiddly i o. Fie, fi, fiddly i o. Fie, fi, fiddly i o" could be replaced by "Be, Bi, Biddly i o" or "We, Wi, Widdly i o." And for "Old MacDonald Had a Farm," the refrain of "E I E I O" could be replace by "B BI B BI BO," "ME, MI, ME, MI, MO," or "NE, NI, NE, NI, NO."

Rhyming Opportunities Are Everywhere

Point to an object in the room and ask the children to say a word that rhymes with it. For example:

- Point to the clock and ask children what they are wearing that rhymes with it. (*sock*)

- Point to a pen and ask what farm animal rhymes with it. (*hen*)

- In a classroom, when there are a few extra minutes at the end of class, throw out a word and ask for words that rhyme with it. I would sometimes dismiss students for lunch or recess as soon as they came up with a rhyming word.

Sometimes healthy competition is helpful. But if this game causes stress, don't make it a condition for them to rhyme. Keep it light and fun! Words that have many rhymes include *nation, head, fly,* and *bee.*

The Name Game

Ask a child to say his or her name. Then repeat the name, pausing between syllables and clapping each one out. If you are in a classroom, ask the rest of the children to join in: "Priya. Pri [with a clap] ya [with a clap]." Then go to the next child, who will say his name, and clap out the syllables with him. Be sure the students can put the name back together. The sequence would go: "Tommy." "Tom-my [with claps]. Then "Tommy" again. With a large class, do a few names each day.

I Spy with My Little Eye

This is a favorite with the younger set. Look around the room and find an easily rhymed word. Then say, "I spy with my little eye [a good rhyming phrase] something that rhymes with *hot*." (Perhaps you have a flower pot in the room.) A child comes up with an answer that rhymes and then takes the role of finding an object and saying, "I spy with my little eye ..." In a classroom, have students raise their hands to give the answer.

Taking Off

Using words from any story that you have read with your child or children, say that you are going to take off sounds. For instance, if you take off the /r/ sound in *rice*, you get *ice*. For example, ask them what you get if you take off the /h/ in *hat*. Then go through several words from the story. Have children help you think of words, and you can have them take turns taking off sounds.

Word Wall

In the classroom or at home, put up new words each week on a word wall. The number of words will depend on the grade level you teach. As I travel the country and observe in classes from kindergarten through high school, I see word walls at every level. With a younger class, practice saying the words, spelling the words, clapping out syllables, and breaking the words into phonemes. Here are a few more word wall activities:

Find two words that rhyme with _____.
Which word means _____?
Find words that end with _____.

Older students can find rhyming words or use the words in conversation.

The important element for struggling readers is that they hear the sounds in the words and say them correctly. Word walls are an excellent way to help build vocabulary at every grade level, a topic discussed in more detail in chapter 7.

Oll Call

In this activity for the classroom, when you ask students to line up, explain that you are going to do so by calling them up individually, a process often called taking roll or roll call. In this game, you will be taking off the first letter of their name and see if the class can tell you what sound is missing. So Jamal would be Amal, and students should tell you that the missing sound is "j." Hence, the game isn't roll call; it's oll call!

Mother, May I?

One of my favorite childhood games can be made into a phonemic awareness game. Children stand in a horizontal line in a designated area many feet from the adult. The adult begins by stating a child's name and telling him or her to take a specific number of steps forward:

You: Byron, take two steps forward.
Bryon: Mother, may I?
You: Yes, you may if you can step out the sounds in the word *at*.

With this Byron begins taking one step and saying /a/ and the second step saying /t/.

Proceed to the next child in line. If a child is unable to give the sounds in the word, he or she must stay in place. You can give the child an easier word in the next round. A winner is declared when one of the children reaches the adult.

Summary

Understanding that spoken words are made of individual sounds is an important foundational skill for literacy and should develop in early childhood. An example of phonemic awareness includes realizing that the word *ball* is made of three sounds: b/a/l/. Phonemic awareness is more likely to develop in children who have varied language experiences, including word play activities such as rhyming and singing activities. Many children develop phonemic awareness easily and without explicit instruction, while others may need repeated exposure to activities that help make this connection. Since this is such an important skill for later literacy development, parents and preschool providers need to provide the experiences that foster phonemic awareness. It is also important that teachers be aware that struggling readers may lack phonemic awareness. When the brain areas for phonemic awareness are developed, it is prime time to begin the process of playing with sounds, which following chapter explores.

CHAPTER 5

Patterns and Programs and Phonics! Oh, My!

T HAT PHONICS CHANGES BRAINS WAS THE conclusion reached after a land-
mark study at Yale School of Medicine in 2004 (Shaywitz et al.,
2004). Direct, systematic, and focused instruction changes struggling readers' brains so they look much like the brains of normal
readers. Add to that conclusion "and enhances intelligence."

The scientific research indicates that most children need phonics
to learn to read. Remember that there is no reading pathway
in the brain until it is made through neuronal recycling. The
brain's natural plasticity makes many things possible, including
changes that can transform a struggling reader into a successful
one (Dehaene, 2009).

In this chapter, we look at how the brain learns and processes
patterns and programs and uses them to identify words and sound
them out. Pattern and program recognition allow the brain to take
new information and store it according to familiar configurations.
Notice that the words *pattern* and *program* begin with /p/ and make
the regular sound of /p/, but the word *phonics*, which also begins
with /p/, does not have the same sound. Until a child learns that
/ph/ sounds like /f/, he will mispronounce the word as he uses the
learned pattern. His brain is trying to make sense out of confusion.
Once he stores the /ph/ pattern, the mistake is corrected.

Patterns are the recognizable units that are stored, and programs
are the step-by-step processes children follow to match new learning
to old—for example:

Pattern: The child sees the word *l-o-g* and knows how to pronounce *d-o-g*, so she pronounces *log* correctly.

Program: The child now has a program that appears reliable: see a word that ends in /og/ and pronounce it like *dog* and *log*.

Patterns and Programs

Hints on Pronunciation for Foreigners

I take it you already know of tough and bough and cough and dough?
Others may stumble but not you, on hiccough, thorough, laugh, and through.
Well done! And now you wish, perhaps, to learn of less familiar traps?
Beware of heard, a dreadful word that looks like beard and sounds like bird,
And dead: it's said like bed, not bead – for goodness' sake don't call it "deed"!
Watch out for meat and great and threat (they rhyme with suite and straight and debt).
A moth is not a moth in mother nor both in bother, broth in brother,
And here is not a match for there nor dear and fear for bear and pear,
And then there's dose and rose and lose—just look them up—and goose and choose,
And cork and work and card and ward, and font and front and word and sword,
And do and go and thwart and cart—come, come, I've hardly made a start!
A dreadful language? Man alive. I'd mastered it when I was five!

Unknown author (from Adams, 1990)

This poem illustrates the frustration of learning to read and follow the rules of English. Other languages often have a consistent letter-to-sound correlation. Although most of the literature states that the English language has forty-four phonemes, there are more than a thousand ways that they can be represented. As a result, English has words that have the same sounds but are spelled differently, words that are spelled the same but pronounced differently, words that contain letters that have nothing to do with the way the words are pronounced, and words that contain silent letters. English spelling rules have lists of many exceptions—words that do not follow the rules and thus must be memorized separately. Table 5.1 illustrates these points.

The brain learns through patterning. Phonemic awareness, as discussed in chapter 4, is a subgroup of phonological awareness that focuses specifically on recognizing and manipulating phonemes, the smallest units of sound. Phonics is another area of phonological awareness that requires students to know and match letters or letter patterns with sounds, learn the rules of spelling, and use this information to decode (read) and encode

Table 5.1 Some Confusing Examples of English Spelling

Pattern	Examples	Pronunciations
ight	light, right, might, height	Long *i* sound plus *t* sound
Words that sound the same but are spelled differently	seen, scene hear, here	Long *e* sound plus *n* Long *e* sound plus *r*
Silent letters	know, knee write, wrist doubt, debt	Pronounced as though the first letter is not there Pronounced as though the *b* is not there
Words that are spelled the same but pronounced differently	read (present tense) read (past tense)	Long *e* Short *e*
Words containing *oo* spelling but pronounced differently	foot, flood	Flood: schwa sound (flud) Foot: short oo sound

(write) words. Phonological awareness involves recognizing and learning patterns, remembering patterns, and matching words to those patterns. Keep in mind as you read this chapter that the brain searches for patterns in order to make sense of the world.

I was reminded recently by a friend, Robert Sylwester (personal communication, September 30, 2011), one of the pioneers in translating brain research, of the following paragraph that made many rounds through the Internet over the past several years:

> Aoccdrnig to a rscheearch at Cmabrigde Uinervtisy, it deosn't mttaer in waht oredr the ltteers in a wrod are, the olny iprmoetnt tihng is taht the frist and lsat ltteer be at the rghit pclae. The rset can be a total mses and you can sitll raed it wouthit porbelm. Tihs is bcuseae the huamn mnid deos not raed ervey lteter by istlef, but the wrod as a wlohe. Amzanig huh?
>
> PS: hwo'd you like to run this by your sepll ckehcer?

I have shown this to many audiences who were able to easily read it. Bob explained why this is so (Sylwester, 2011). Proficient readers read most words by looking at the first and last letters as well as noting the general shape of the word. We often read misspelled words with little difficulty due to this pattern of reading.

We know from previous chapters that written language (reading) is processed through various areas of the brain found principally in the left hemisphere. And we are aware that reading must be taught explicitly due to the lack of a genetic program like the one available for speech. Reading the written word is possible due to the brain's use of the object recognition system. For beginning readers, words take on familiar shapes and are stored as objects. By comparing these patterns, the brain is able to make sense of what it sees (Dehaene, 2009). Challenge your brain with the following paragraph:

7H15 M3554G3 53RV35 7O PR0V3 H0W 0UR M1ND5 C4N D0 4M4Z1NG 7H1NG5! 1MPR3551V3 7H1NG5! 1N 7H3 B3G1NN1NG 17 WA5 H4RD BU7 N0W, 0N 7H15 LIN3 Y0UR M1ND 1S R34D1NG 17 4U70M471C4LLY W17H 0U7 3V3N 7H1NK1NG 4B0U7 17, B3 PROUD! 0NLY C3R741N P30PL3 C4N R3AD 7H15.

You were probably able to break the code for this paragraph in a line or two. Your brain may have balked a bit at the beginning of the first sentence, but it was able to identify the patterns. Although this paragraph is a bit more challenging than the previous one, your brain searched for meaning and found it. Had it not recognized any patterns, it could have made no sense of the paragraph, and you would quickly have forgotten the information.

Making sense of letters and text requires the activation of several brain areas. The visual cortex (the occipital lobe) is activated as the brain views the words. Initially those words are stored as pictures in the object area of the visual cortex. It is this area that, according to Dehaene (2009), is recycled into the word form area. He goes on to conclude that we learn to read because we have inherited a proficient and efficient object recognition system that is plastic (*neuroplasticity* refers to the brain's ability to change) enough to add new shapes and objects (those word shapes). Once these areas are also linked to the language areas of the brain, the reading pathway is created.

Reading dates back five thousand years and is not only a cognitive activity but also a social and cultural one. The ways of learning to read vary. Yet whether you learned to read by filling out phonics worksheets, tracing letters in sand or shaving cream, reading the Dick and Jane series, or were taught through the whole word

Phonics Versus Whole Language

What about the controversy between phonics and whole language? Whole language advocates dislike phonics: they believe phonics teaches words out of context and that this method does not lead to comprehension. Research showed, however, that children developed many inaccuracies from the whole language approach. Whole language relies on children memorizing words rather than sounding them out, and without phonics, there are just too many words to memorize. Whole language advocates believe there are too many irregularities in pronunciation, so, they say, phonics rules are unreliable.

When reading scores plummeted in some states, including California, whole language was considered the culprit, and the National Reading Panel influenced most states to return to the phonics approach in 2000 (Dehaene, 2009). Most districts now seek a balance between the two methods: they have learned that no one strategy works for every child.

approach, the locations of brain areas activated for reading are identical.

The Alphabetic Principle

The alphabetic principle states that spoken words are made up of sounds (phonemes) that are represented in written form (letters). Through phonemic awareness training, the brain stores the sounds of the letters.

Many children first learn to recognize the letter symbols, that is, their ABCs, called graphemes. Identifying the sounds that each of the letters represent is the next step in learning to read. The words in the ''Hints on Pronunciation for Foreigners,'' the poem earlier in this chapter, are just some of the many that cause brain problems for English learners. Remember that the brain remembers patterns, so words such as *dead* and *bead* often confuse new readers.

One to One? Not Exactly

"The reading process is driven by the visual recognition of individual letters in familiar ordered sequence and is critically supported by the translation of those strings of letters into their phonological correspondences," writes Adams (1990, p. 237). In other words, in order for children to learn to read, they must not only recognize letters but also be able to apply their sounds. That sounds much simpler, and it would be easier if our letters did not have so many sounds and if our sounds did not have so many letters.

For example, four-year-old Emily wonders why *k-a-t* doesn't spell *cat,* why *circus* doesn't begin with an *s,* and how you're supposed to pronounce the word *knee.* Emily is beginning to read, but the process is very slow as she sounds out words that can't be sounded out.

To see what Emily is up against, here's an experiment to try. Your task is to pronounce the following word: *ghoti.* In fact, *ghoti* is a respelling of the word *fish* using this pronunciation:

gh, pronounced /f/ as in *tough*

o, pronounced /i/ as in *women*

ti, pronounced /sh/ as in *nation*

The fact is that even the word *phonetically* isn't spelled phonetically.

The Common Core: Where Do We Stand with the Standards?

Just as with phonemic awareness, you will find phonics standards in the Common Core Reading Standards under "Foundational

Skills." Standard 3 from grades K through 5 states that students should "know and apply grade-level phonics and word analysis skills in decoding words" (Common Core State Standards, 2010, pp. 16–17).

At the kindergarten level, students need to demonstrate basic knowledge of one-to-one letter-sound correspondence by generating many of the most frequent sounds for each consonant, associate long and short sounds with common spellings (graphemes) for the five major vowels, read common high-frequency words by sight, and distinguish among similarly spelled words by identifying the sounds of the letters that differ.

Grade 1 students are expected to know the spelling-sound correspondences for common consonant digraphs, decode regularly spelled one-syllable words, know final *e* and common vowel team conventions for representing long vowel sounds (I know that words ending in silent *e* and two vowels together can make the vowel long), use knowledge that every syllable must have a vowel sound to determine the number of syllables in a printed word, decode two-syllable words following basic patterns by breaking the words into syllables, read words with inflectional endings, and be able to recognize and read grade-appropriate irregularly spelled words.

Phonics standards continue to increase with higher expectations through grade 5, at which time students should be able to use their combined knowledge of all letter-sound correspondences, syllabication patterns, and morphology to accurately read unfamiliar multisyllabic words in context and out of context.

Decoding Development in the Brain

Beginning around the age of five, the left hemisphere shows an increase in dendritic growth in Broca's area, the speech center located in the frontal lobe (Kagan & Herschkowitz, 2005). This may be the final year of such massive growth, as by the age of six, most brains are showing a stronger dendritic pattern in the right hemisphere. According to Elias and Arnold (2006), age five may be the developmental time when internal language (i.e., the inner voice or thought) develops. This is an important advancement, because reading comprehension relies on verbal and visual memory (Brookes, 2006). Other changes are taking place in the brain as well:

- The frontal lobes begin to communicate more easily as the anterior corpus callosum continues to myelinate. Although the frontal lobes are not fully developed until the mid-twenties, massive connectivity is going on in the early years (Kagan & Herschkowitz, 2005).

- The myelination process continues throughout the limbic system (Kagan & Herschkowitz, 2005). The structures in the limbic system include the amygdala (the emotional center) and the hippocampus (the structure necessary for the creation of long-term memories).

- In the back and at the top of the brain (the parietal and temporal lobes), myelin increases. As reading and vocabulary develop dramatically, the connection between these lobes is vital (Kagan & Herschkowitz, 2005). The myelin helps signals travel quickly and accurately.

- Chemical levels in the brain increase, with dopamine reaching close to adult levels. This allows children to focus and concentrate more (Berk, 2001). Beyond these attributes, dopamine is released when the brain feels good about something, like reaching a goal. We hope that learning to read for anyone at any age will feel like an important accomplishment. Then dopamine will be discharged by the nucleus accumbens, a small structure in the limbic brain that regularly releases dopamine but sends even more of this feel-good chemical to the prefrontal cortex for a job well done. The brain loves dopamine and remembers what it has done in order to receive a large amount. Therefore, it wants to do it again (Willis, 2011).

Decoding letters into their sounds involves the left temporal lobe, especially its superior regions. These are also associated with the analysis of speech sounds. Letters and sounds first meet in this area of the brain. Brain imaging techniques show that the visual areas of the brain become activated by letter shapes and auditory areas by the sounds of those letters. As a child begins to decode letters, such as *d* and *a*, and create the sound *da*, the planum temporale, part of Wernicke's area that is an auditory motor system, receives the letter shapes and the speech sounds and creates a relationship between them (Dehaene, 2009). With practice, the letter-to-sound (phoneme-to-grapheme) translation becomes automatic. It is the automaticity that allows a reader to read and comprehend what he or she is reading.

Let's look at Jack, who is now in kindergarten. He began reading at age three and a half. He sounded out words and with some assistance was successful. Now Jack is learning sight words. He is quite good at it and is encouraged to read second-grade books. He does this handily, yet the thrill of recognizing words by sight causes him some frustration when new words that need to be sounded out show up in his reading books. This response is not uncommon as the brain switches from the automatic pathway and begins to use the more laborious program of assigning sound to letter, combining those sounds and discovering a word.

When the brain encounters a word repeatedly, it builds neural networks for the spelling, pronunciation, and the meaning of the word. Scientists believe that a model of this word that includes the information in all of these networks will eventually be formed and stored in the area of the brain referred to as the word form area. This resides in the area of the brain where the occipital lobe and temporal lobe meet. Dehaene has dubbed this area "the brain's letterbox" (2009). It is through explicit phonics instruction that these word form networks are created.

Phonics Instruction

There are several forms of phonics instruction that teach the letter-sound relationship in an explicit, systematic way. You may be teaching phonics using any of the following approaches:

- *Analogy based*—uses parts of word families to identify unknown words that have similar parts

- *Analytic*—analyzes letter-sound relationships in words that are already known

- *Embedded*—exposes children to phonics as examples become available in text

- *Onset-rime phonics*—identifies sounds before the first vowel (onset) and then addresses the rest of the word (the rime)

- *Phonics through spelling*—segments words into phonemes and then develops new words using the phonemes that have been learned

- *Synthetic phonics*—converts letters or combinations of letters into sounds and then blends sounds for words that are recognizable

Effective phonics programs contain instruction that:

- Offers systematic and explicit instruction

- Builds understanding for children about the relationship between sounds and letters

- Is adaptable to individual children's needs

- Allows children to apply phonics skills as they read

- Includes components related to learning alphabetic knowledge, phonemic awareness, vocabulary, and the reading of text (Wolfe & Neville, 2009)

Factors That Lead to Learning

In my book *How to Teach So Students Remember* (2005), I refer to the factors of learning (Arendal & Mann, 2000), which can be applied in any teaching situation and will affect the outcome of student learning:

- *Frequency.* Neural pathways need to build and grow strong by repeated exposure to the learning. In reading, studies have shown that the more a person reads, the better that person will read. Similarly, if you lift weights only occasionally, you will not build up your muscles. But if you lift regularly, you will accomplish your desired fitness level.

- *Intensity.* Learning requires rigorous practice. A child can build neural support for the skill in a shorter period of time if she practices intensely. As athletes prepare themselves for competitions, their workouts become more and more intense.

- *Cross training.* Teaching for memory requires strong networks that can connect to other networks. Therefore, different kinds of skills and different learning styles should be addressed.

- *Adaptivity.* Progress monitoring is required to adjust the teaching and learning to meet the needs of all students. It is through assessment that teaching can be differentiated.

- *Motivation and attention.* These factors are what keep students interested in their learning. Although phonics should be systematic and sequential, children should be motivated through various means. Excitement can be contagious.

Eenie, Meenie, Minee, Moe. Or Is It Eeny, Meany, Miny, Mo?

When family members arrived for a holiday get-together, they found the sign in figure 5.1 taped to the front door. This is an example of invented spelling. When children don't know how to spell a word correctly, they use their letter-sound knowledge to create the word as it sounds. Can you read the sign? ''Welcome to the Christmas party.''

Invented spelling is a prereading skill. Sarah Ahmed and Linda Lombardino (2000) found that invented spelling is an accurate measure of reading achievement. Reading and writing are closely

❖ FIGURE 5.1: *Invented Spelling Example*

linked. Five-year-old Jack, whose idea it was to make the sign in figure 5.1, was excited about his ability to read and connect sounds and letters. His parents often find items around the house labeled with sticky notes or index cards. It is this excitement about learning to read that helps motivate children and thrills teachers and parents as they watch.

As students advance from simple to complex reading rules, their spelling improves. According to Bear, Invernizzi, Templeton, & Johnston (2008), there are five stages of spelling development:

Stage 1: Emergent (preliterate). At this stage, which covers ages three through five, children often string letters together, but they don't associate the marks with any specific phonemes. This is a time for a natural expression of spelling and words. At the beginning of this stage, emergent spellers may not write from left to right, but by the end of the stage, they usually do. They typically learn to make letters, learn the letter-sound connection, and learn the direction of writing.

Stage 2: Letter name–alphabetic spelling. This is often the stage of invented spelling in which children are familiar with phonemes and write the sounds that they hear. From ages five to seven, children learn the alphabetic principle, become familiar with consonant and short vowel sounds, and begin to learn consonant blends and digraphs.

Stage 3: Within-word pattern spelling. At this stage, children are usually seven to nine years old and learn to spell most one-syllable short-vowel words. They also learn to spell long-vowel patterns and *r*-controlled vowels. Children may reverse the order of letters (such as writing *brun* for *burn*) and mix up spelling patterns (such as writing *swete* instead of *sweet*).

Stage 4: Syllables and affixes spelling. Children focus on syllables and apply what they've learned about one-syllable words to longer multisyllabic words. From nine to eleven years old, they learn about inflectional endings (*-s, -es, -ed, -ing*) and the rules for adding those endings. They also understand syllabication and homophones. It is helpful to work with them on which words change *y* to *i* or when to drop the final *e* before adding a suffix.

Stage 5: Derivational relations spelling. Children between eleven and fourteen years old explore the relationship between spelling and meaning during the derivational relations stage. This is the stage of understanding and studying root words and Greek and Latin derivations. Some children find it fun to see how words are transformed with prefixes and suffixes. For instance, the word *locate* can be changed to *location* or *relocate*, and they can discuss how these transformations change the part of speech and the meaning.

Of course, brains develop at different ages, and these stages and ages are only averages. Students' spelling is indicative of their understanding of orthography, phonics, and the spelling patterns they have learned. The invented spelling indicates the concepts or patterns they haven't mastered. Keep in mind that although some teachers believe that invented spelling reinforces bad habits, the research suggests otherwise.

Activities

The activities that follow are for parents and teachers to help children recognize the sounds of language, hear patterns in words, and model the enjoyment of reading and language.

Reading Aloud

Because research strongly supports the importance of listening to a fluent reader read aloud, children of all ages should be read to every day. There are many reasons for this:

- They can see and hear that someone enjoys reading.

- They can hear the patterns in the words.

- They learn a higher level of vocabulary than they will in their own books.

- They learn to pay attention.

Play Rhyming Games

This is a good activity for parents when they are in the car with their children. Simply think of a word and ask for one that rhymes. Like reading aloud, this activity has no age limits.

Shaping Up

With younger children who are having difficulty seeing patterns, practice with using shapes. Draw a pattern—perhaps a square, triangle, square, triangle—and then ask what shape comes next. With older children, make the pattern more difficult by specifying three or four shapes.

Play Homonym Games

Asking kids how many meanings there are to a word (e.g., *jam*) promotes discussion about words. Then have them think of a word with multiple meanings. You can talk about syllables, sounds, and rhyming words as well. This activity is fun in the classroom and at home.

Multisyllable Alphabet Words

This is a great classroom game or one to play after dinner. Have the child write the alphabet in a list on the left side of a piece of paper. Then ask him to write at least a two-syllable word for each letter. You can use a theme, such as food, video games, television shows, book titles, or anything else that may come to mind or that the child is studying at school.

Purple Penguins

This game, which uses words that all begin with the same sound (e.g., "Purple penguins pick pineapples") can be played in class-rooms and with your own children (Kaye, 1984). Make up a sentence and say it to the child and see if she can tell if it is a true Purple Penguin. For instance, "Happy hamsters eat ham" does not meet the criteria because *eat* does not begin with an *h*. This is a great way to get kids thinking about sounds and patterns.

Summary

Most of the literature suggests using a strong phonics program when teaching reading to most students. But balance is important. Even if you are using a whole language approach, keep in mind that the brain needs to make connections and recycle those neurons for a strong reading pathway. That is why an explicit, sequential program is important. Once children have a strong background in phonemic awareness and phonics, our work with them on fluency begins.

CHAPTER 6

The Fluent Reader

A T A RECENT BIRTHDAY PARTY, I ASKED one seven-year-old how school was going. His quick reply was, "I like recess and gym." This response took me immediately back to my middle school teaching days and the usual comeback parents and I would get from many of the boys. Those children usually were having difficulty of some kind at school. It may have been social, but often it was reading related. The students who felt successful almost always had a favorite subject, a favorite teacher (who made them feel successful), or strong social ties. Girls most often had a positive response, even if it was strongly socially prompted.

But that was middle school. A seven-year-old's response gave me pause for thought. However, I did not have to think very long, for as soon as the boy had wandered away to play with some other children, his parents brought me up to speed on his reaction and his progress. "He got a 2 in fluency," one of them told me. I truly did not know what the meaning of "2" was for this child at his school, and I must have looked somewhat confused. "That's a 2 out of 5," his mother explained. "And it's based on this ridiculous test," his father chimed in. "Even the teacher thinks it's a bad test."

"Well, how *is* his reading?" I queried. I knew this conversation was not going to end without some comment from me.

"He hesitates between words. His verbal skills are excellent, but he doesn't seem to know how to read smoothly and with emphasis in the right places," his dad added.

"Is that what you find at home when he reads aloud to you?" I asked. With that question, the mother and father looked at each other and Mom hurriedly piped in, "He doesn't really like to read, but since he got the 2, he has begun asking to read with us."

Alarms went off in my head and red flags popped up. These were very bright thirty-somethings who had graduated with honors from universities with master's degrees and passed the CPA exam. I knew they had gone to all of the right Web sites about child rearing and helping kids succeed. But something was surely missing.

"So, are you telling me that you haven't been reading to him or that he just isn't interested in reading to you?"

"Last year [that would have been first grade]," Mom offered, "he said they did enough reading at school and he didn't want to read at night. He wanted to play games . . . educational games that really helped him with spatial skills and strategies."

What I believe I am hearing is that at some point, these two bright parents stopped reading aloud to their child. At what point is that okay? Never. Even if my children are twenty-two, if they're in my house, there's going to be some reading aloud going on. As crazy as that may sound, we never outgrow the need and the desire to share information. I won't be reading storybooks to my twenty-somethings, but I will be sharing articles, Web sites, cartoons, and any other thought-provoking and fun interaction that revolves in some way around reading.

Through continued conversation with the parents, I discovered that although they began reading to him from infancy, school changed his desire to be read to. In a school setting, somehow being read to was equated with the knowledge that he must learn to read, perhaps changing this bright child's perception of the reason behind reading. When his parents "let the reading" slide, some of the magic associated with it may have disappeared. The fact that the 2 he received is somehow motivating him to want to read may be competitively based. Competition is sometimes positive motivation, but we must keep in mind that reading is not genetically based. It takes real work, which can and should be fun, to change those neural connections—to borrow neurons from nearby networks and create a reading pathway.

Fluent reading is often defined as fast, smooth, effortless, and automatic reading of text, whether silent or out loud, with attention focused on the meaning of the text. Because fluency is the ability to read quickly and easily at an automatic level, it does not necessarily translate into being a comprehensive reader. That is the second part of fluency: the ability to decode words, understand their meaning, and add the inflection because you understand what you are reading. Internationally known author and literacy specialist Regie Routman (2003) tells us that students who read fluently without understanding are not truly reading but rather are "word calling."

Strong neural connections influence reading speed and accuracy. In this chapter, we look at strategies that increase fluency in a brain-compatible manner.

What Fluency Means

Fluency is a process by which the ability to decode words is bridged to comprehension. Without fluency, the words on the page do not come to life and become meaningful to readers.

Interventions have been shown to help struggling readers, including those diagnosed with dyslexia. These intervention programs usually begin by focusing on phonemic awareness, the ability to hear sounds and manipulate them, as well as their association with their graphic representations, letters. One area that often remains problematic is fluency. The majority of children with reading difficulties may end up reading at an adequate level, but not necessarily at grade level. Their decoding skills and comprehension are strengthened, but their fluency is not addressed (Dehaene, 2009).

Ask most reading experts what helps children learn to read, and the answer is simple, if not easy: children learn to read by reading. Problem readers often lack the time with print that most normal readers do. The problem of children like the boy in the opening story—those who have developed the reading pathway and whose brains have been changed but still don't read fluently—may be their lack of contact with print. The more they read, the more fluent they become.

Let's take another look at the definition of *fluency*. Most people describe fluency as the ability to read accurately and quickly. Along with that definition is the ability to read with expression and without effort, and as they read aloud, they divide words into phrases that make sense within the framework of the text. This all sounds very reasonable. As mature readers, we know that we do all of this as we read and at the same time understand what we are reading. It is this understanding that allows us to put emphasis on the correct group of words, even on the correct syllable, as we determine what definition of a word is used in a particular text. (For instance, in the sentence, "I didn't know that she said that," the reader must figure out whether the emphasis goes on the word *she* or the word *that*.)

As a reading and literature teacher, I have found that although good readers in most cases are able to handle text in this manner, there are exceptions. Children who are learning to read are often asked to read aloud. In fact, several reading fluency and comprehension tests ask a child to do a cold oral reading (i.e., read text they have never read before) fluently and then answer questions about the content. In some studies, however, brain scans suggest that during oral reading, there is more brain activity in the speech centers, indicating perhaps that the student is concentrating more on the impression he or she is making to the audience. Silent reading shows more activity in the prefrontal cortex, an area associated with higher-level thinking and working memory. It may be that students who are reading aloud, especially text that is new to them, do not comprehend very much. Therefore, testing fluency as well as comprehension in this fashion may be unreliable.

I can recall reading aloud to my classes, sometimes a piece of literature unfamiliar to me. My fluency would sometimes be challenged by my inexperience with some of the context, and I would have to repeat a sentence or phrase in order to emphasize appropriately. Fortunately, I was modeling a good reading strategy for my students.

The Brain's Pathway to Fluency

According to Willis (2008), "Fluent readers can decode, recognize, and comprehend the meaning of text at the same time, so their networks fire effectively and efficiently" (p. 47). One of the prerequisites to this marvelous feat is the myelination of several neural networks. One of the questions has always been, "Is myelination a result of brain development or of use?" Those who believe that it belongs in the "use it or lose it" category might encourage a child to read before the brain systems are ready. Knowing when a child is ready to read could be crucial to both future success with reading and developing a love of reading and learning. Signs that a child is ready to read include interest and motivation. Is the child excited about reading time? Do you find the child curious about books? Letter and sound recognition are the next signs. Can the child point out letters in a text, and does he or she have phonemic awareness—knowledge that each letter makes a sound? The brain areas responsible for phonemic awareness must be mature for this to take place.

If a child is required to learn to read at an age when the brain systems necessary have not matured or the connections have not been made, the brain tries to create different pathways to reading that can be cumbersome for the brain. This has been called negative neural wiring and can be compared to getting inappropriate directions when you are headed to a particular destination. For instance, MapQuest may not have up-to-date maps that include detours and road closures, so you spend extra time and extra gas and have added stress trying to reach your journey's end. So it goes with the child trying to read before his or her brain has reached readiness levels. Not only is a less-than-ideal pathway created, but the act of reading is associated with pressure and stress. The automaticity necessary for good fluency is not reached and the expressiveness associated with a good reading is lacking and leads to problems with comprehension. The bottom line is that the child's wiring has been compromised and rewiring will be necessary.

Rewiring begins with removing the stress from reading. This includes the "starting-over" process of reading aloud with no expectations other than enjoyment of the experience. When the child realizes there is no pressure, he or she may begin to try to "read" to you, even though this reading act is memorization of what he or she has heard along with clues from illustrations on the pages. When the child begins to recognize some isolated sounds and words, you will know that the brain is beginning to make the proper connections.

Reading Is Pleasure

This brings us to another important question: How do we involve the brain's attention and pleasure systems in the reading process? We know that involving the pleasure system and bathing the brain in the neurotransmitter dopamine will keep the child focused on the tasks that continue to activate this intrinsic reward (Willis, 2008). As I noted in chapter 1, a love of reading begins when an infant is held lovingly and securely while the primary caregiver reads to the child for the very first time. At that moment, dopamine is released in the infant's pleasure system, awakening a love of reading.

For students who do not struggle with reading, the pleasure continues. Knowing they are fluent readers who read expressively, even impressively, in front of their classmates or others gives them that dopamine rush from the feeling of doing a good job. They feel secure in their ability to read and comprehend. These students can allocate their resources for comprehension.

Students who struggle with fluency are stuck using their mental resources to decode words and try to make sense of them. For these students, reading aloud is an embarrassment, and they may be worried that other students will become impatient or make fun of them. It behooves all teachers to create a safe and secure environment in which all readers feel comfortable doing their best. Many teachers do this by sometimes intentionally making mistakes in front of the students and talking about how everyone makes mistakes. Another way is by sharing classroom rules from the beginning of the school year that the classroom is a place where learning takes place and we learn from trying hard and practicing. In this safe environment, students are also praised for the effort they put forth.

Lev Vygotsky (1978), the famous educational psychologist, developed the zone of proximal development: the difference between what a learner can do without help and what he or she can do with help. We can look at zone of proximal development and ask, "What is the child able to do with a little help?" "What is the child able to do on his or her own?" Pleasure comes from the acquisition of something that elicits a good feeling, which is why dopamine is often called the feel-good neurotransmitter.

High-Frequency and Sight Words

In their book *Practical Fluency: Classroom Perspectives, Grades K-6* (2006), teachers Max Brand and Gail Brand remind us to ask ourselves if our students truly are fluent. Do they read in meaningful phrases, use punctuation to guide their reading, anticipate what will come next, and adjust their reading according to this information? I often wonder if students understand their reading well enough to reread when something is difficult or doesn't make sense. A fluent reader would do all this and more.

Fluent readers need automaticity in sight words (those that do not follow normal decoding rules and must be learned by sight) and high-frequency words (words that appear so commonly in text that students must also know them by sight), and it is important to assess whether your struggling readers know these words (Beers, 2003). Flash cards are a quick and simple way to determine whether children know these words. You can do an Internet search and find several word lists to use to create the flash cards. Often the Dolch Basic Sight Vocabulary words (available at http://www .dolchsightwords.org/) are used in that category, and Fry's Instant Word List (available at http://www.k12reader.com/fry-word-list -1000-high-frequency-words/) is used for high-frequency words. These words can be used on Word Walls, on flash cards, and in word search puzzles to engage students to use these words quickly and easily.

Keep in mind that a child may have trouble with a word out of context and be able to recognize it within a text. However, it is imperative that the students know these words without hesitation in any situation. Their working memories will be too busy decoding difficult words and using comprehension strategies to waste time and brain space on sight words.

Some Steps to Fluency

Children who are fluent readers put their brains on automatic when it comes to decoding and recognizing words. They have practiced reading to the point where their working memories are cleared of the clutter of sounding out words, which offers them the ability to focus on comprehension. To make meaning of text, readers must be able to decode the words on the printed page accurately and automatically and use prosody (expression) when reading.

Table 6.1 Gradual Release of Responsibility for Fluency Model

I do it.	Reading aloud to students
We do it together.	Choral reading
You do it together.	Choral reading without teacher
You do it alone.	Reading alone after practice

Therefore, we will divide fluency into those three components:

- Accurate decoding

- Automatic decoding

- Using prosody

All three of these rely on the reading pathway in the brain: how mature it is, how well set up it is, and how those neuronal connections have been made and maintained.

We can look at the gradual release of responsibility (Pearson & Gallagher, 1983) model when we talk about reading fluency, a four-part approach that leads to independence in the area you are teaching. It always begins with the teacher. The GRR model, as it is often called, is shown in table 6.1.

To begin the process of teaching fluency, we adults are the ones with the control and responsibility. We begin by modeling. The "I do; you watch" step is part of the mirror neuron system in the brain. By watching and listening to how text is read smoothly and with expression, children begin to understand what is expected of a fluent reader. They must see that the reading appears effortless, but we cannot stop there. Fluency leads to comprehension, so during and after our reading, we discuss with them what they might have heard (Rasinksi & Griffith, 2011)—for example:

"Did you hear how I slowed down in certain parts of the text and sped up in others? Why do you think I did that?"

"Did you notice a long pause at one point in the reading? What effect did that have on you as the listener?"

"I emphasized some words during the reading. Did you notice those words? Do you know why I gave some words such emphasis?"

These situations provide children with a clear target in their own reading. They begin to understand that how they read text helps them understand its meaning. Explain to them how reading accurately and automatically with prosody frees up their working memory and allows them to think about the content of the text.

This step in the explicit teaching of fluency may also include readings by the adult while children have a copy of the text and can follow along. In this way, students can see how and why the adult is pacing the reading, as well as accurately reading and using expression.

The "we do it together" step in the GRR model can be done using different strategies. In table 6.1, I suggest choral reading: the adult and child or group of children read a passage together, which allows children to be in sync with the adult and their classmates as they read. (I discuss variations on choral reading at the end of this chapter.) It is important to note that hearing and speaking a word at the same time helps to put that word into long-term memory as a sight word.

If you do not feel comfortable reading a passage or you choose to do observations during this phase of the model, a recording of a passage may be played and children read along with the recorded voice.

"You do it together" is the next phase of the GRR model. At this time children may read a passage together without an adult or a recording as a whole class, in small groups, or in pairs. This is time for repetition and rehearsal that aid in attaining automaticity, accuracy, and prosody. There should be many repeated readings, which will lead to children's reading passages independently as they try out their new ability. As the children become more and more familiar with a passage, their confidence builds.

Eventually the children reach the "you do it alone" part of the model. This is their opportunity to perform and show you (and themselves!) how well they can do. Some children may be willing to perform for the whole class, while others may be more comfortable one-on-one with you or a small group.

Explicit instruction in fluency is ongoing and should be part of the daily routine in every classroom. As students build confidence and become better readers, this will be evident not only in their oral reading skills but also in silent reading. Students must become fluent in all reading situations. As they gain mastery in fluency, there may be changes in the daily routine, but be sure to offer students many different types of text to practice fluency. Mastery could mean longer passages for them to practice, as well as nonfiction and poetry.

A growing body of research confirms that teaching fluency and practicing lead to comprehension and retention in struggling readers (Griffith & Rasinski, 2004).

Activities

The activities that follow are very useful in increasing reading fluency. Many of these can be used at home with parental support.

Choral Reading

In choral reading, groups of children read passages aloud. They do this multiple times in some type of group formation (whole, small, triads, dyads). If you are grouping, you may have each group read a different part of the passage. You may then change the section of the passage that a group reads so they hear how the passage sounds when another small group reads it. Most children enjoy choral reading, improve their fluency, and read more prosodically in these situations.

Echo Reading

Echo reading is useful for struggling readers and English language learners. For this strategy, a leader reads a line, and the class or group repeats the same line. This allows students who read slowly or word by word to hear how the selection should be read, and they can repeat it immediately.

Antiphonal Choral Reading

Rasinski and Griffith (2011) call this strategy "Readers' Theater with training wheels."

Children are divided into at least two groups, and the text is divided into sections, with each group given a section to read. The groups practice their parts before the whole group is brought together for the performance (or dress rehearsal). You may use a poem to practice this type of reading in which each group has a line to read. "Father William" by Lewis Carroll is a poem I used with my middle school students that worked well for antiphonal choral reading.

Readers' Theater

In Readers' Theater, children have lines of a script taken from a familiar text. The children themselves write the script from a book or story they have read or read a script prepared for them. There are many scripts available online. One of my favorites is http://www.thebestclass.org/rtscripts.html.

Fluency is the hallmark of this strategy because the story is read like a play, but usually there are few props and little movement. It is the prosody that makes the characters come to life. There is no memorization; the children simply hold and read the scripts. Students typically enjoy this strategy whether they write the script from a book or story they have read or if the script is given to them. The text becomes meaningful and fun as the children use their voices and gestures to define their characters.

Cumulative Choral Reading

For this type of reading, one child or group begins the reading, and another child or group joins in as the next passage is read. Children enjoy this type of reading. It can also be reversed so an entire group begins the selection, and with each passage or line, some of them stop reading. At the end, a single child or group is reading.

Reading to Younger Children

Have older children read aloud to younger ones. You or they choose a book at their independent reading level. The children will have to practice reading fluently before they read aloud.

Summary

The best way to increase fluency is through frequent practice. If you are a parent, be sure you are reading aloud to your children and they are reading aloud to you. Listen without comment, and if your child asks you to read the selection aloud, say it is okay to make mistakes and reread with more expression or with proper punctuation. If you are a teacher, have your students read aloud to their parents as well as to the class. When students are practicing for performances of any kind, having an audience is helpful.

In primary classrooms, make "I can do it" cards with short selections on them. Get your faculty and staff involved. Ask them if they would be willing to listen to a student read—without correcting them—at different times during the day. For instance, check ahead of time with the librarian, secretary, custodian, lunch director, principal, or anyone else in the building who may have a few minutes to listen to a student read. When a student has some extra time, offer her a reading selection to practice in class or at home. Then at some later time, give the student a hall pass and tell her to take her card to the person who has agreed to listen to the passage and is available at that time. The student is to politely ask this person if he or she has time to listen to her read. In this way, fluency becomes home and whole school efforts.

CHAPTER 7

Building Vocabulary

V OCABULARY REVIEW BECAME VERY SUCCESSFUL IN my seventh-grade class-room when I began to play vocabulary games with my students. Each student had a partner who sometimes was self-chosen and other times selected by me. The students sat knee to knee, with one student facing the projection screen and the other facing the back wall. As soon as everyone was ready, I projected vocabulary words on the screen. The partner who could see the screen gave clues to his or her partner to identify each word. As soon as the partner got all of the words, the pair raised their hands. This allowed me to see which pair "won" and also keep track of who was finished and who needed more time. If there was a time crunch, I might stop and debrief the students as soon as one pair won the game. When we had the time, I let the game go until each pair finished. In debriefing the students, we discussed which of the definitions allowed the students who were guessing to think of the word quickly.

This was a review activity, not an introduction to the words. I have tried this game both ways and find the review works out for two reasons: there is less pressure because the students have an opportunity to access their prior knowledge, and my students made a point of learning their vocabulary words so as not to disappoint their partners. We thus reviewed twice: in the game itself and then debriefing and discussing good definitions for the words.

I also taught vocabulary words explicitly before the students encountered them in their text. This strategy, along with others shared in this chapter, helped students learn the words, their definitions, synonyms, and antonyms.

Two Types of Vocabulary

We have two types of vocabularies: our receptive vocabulary (words that we read or hear and understand) and our expressive vocabulary (words that we use when we write or speak). We add to both vocabularies by learning new words through listening to others, reading, and direct instruction.

According to Marzano and Kendall (1996), 85 percent of all standardized test scores in all subject areas are dependent on students knowing the vocabulary of the standards. They note that standards, both state and core, contain specific vocabulary that is used in standardized tests. But many students are not familiar with these words, and so reading and understanding exactly what the questions are asking is difficult, and students might select incorrect responses. This is not because they cannot do the computations or know the material, but because the words are meaningless to them. At Turning Point Learning Center School in Emporia, Kansas, this information was put to the test. Melissa Reed, assistant professor of literacy, and undergraduate student Lacy Jordan from Teachers College at Emporia State University conducted a research project with middle school math students. They worked on math terminology and formulas in between testing sessions, and in comparing the pretest and posttest scores, they found that these students performed much better on the posttest (Springer, 2011).

That vocabulary building increases background knowledge is vital information for every parent and educator. Scientific research suggests certain steps to take in explicitly teaching vocabulary. This chapter reviews those steps and offers strategies to make learning words and their meanings desirable to the brain.

Students from poverty often come to school with only half the vocabulary of middle-class students (Marzano & Kendall, 1996). How does this come to be? Vocabulary is built through personal interactions with people, places, things, and ideas, and in many cases, middle-class children have more of these experiences or at least more elaborate experiences. Prior to their years of formal education, many children are having books read to them, which increases vocabularies. Children's speaking and listening vocabularies also vary greatly according to their prior experiences.

Vocabulary Development

By the age of two, most children have between one hundred and two hundred words in their vocabularies. They are also forming simple sentences or phrases that consist of two or three words (Wolfe & Neville, 2004). A two-year-old might say, for example, "All gone" or "Dada home." These phrases are part of the general conversations that they have been hearing on a regular basis.

Between the ages of two and three as the brain continues with its incredibly fast neural connections in the language pathway, sentences can become longer and more complex. Since these early years are great windows of opportunity for learning language, the more a child is spoken to and read to, the greater the chance he or she has for developing an increased vocabulary. Most children start first grade with a vocabulary of about six thousand words, and many add another three thousand words every year through third grade.

An important piece of information emerged from work by Hart and Risley (2003): between 86 and 98 percent of children's recorded vocabularies matched the vocabularies of their parents, whose words were also recorded. By age three, children living in professional families had a recorded vocabulary size of 1,116 words with average utterances per hour of 310. Children in working-class families had a recorded vocabulary size of 749 words with average utterances per hour of 223. And welfare children had a recorded vocabulary size of only 525 words with a mere 168 utterances per hour (Hart & Risley, 2003). This difference over three years would be 45 million words for the child in a professional family versus only 13 million words for the child living in poverty. Thus, as early as age three, there would be an estimated 30 million to 32 million word gap between children in professional families and those living in poverty.

As we look at the vast differences in student vocabulary, research has shown that this gap is meaningful. There is a vast difference in the vocabularies of high-achieving and low-achieving students.

The reading brain has organized itself in such a way that there are networks for the way the word is formed, its spelling, its meaning, and its pronunciation. As a student silently reads a word on a page, a cascade of neural connections provides all the information the student knows about the word (Shaywitz, 2003). The more background knowledge a child has—in this case, the number of words the child knows—the easier it is for him or her to successfully tackle the job of reading and comprehending.

The richness of the neural networks of words is revealed where the occipital lobe and temporal lobe meet. We must include the frontal lobe in the experience of reading words as well. In order to understand which meaning of the word applies, higher-level thinking is needed for attention and decision making. In the case of unknown words, the frontal lobe will also come into play to try various strategies to find meaning.

How do children add words to their mental lexicon? It begins with their listening to conversations in the early environment. Then vocabulary can be added through listening to adults read aloud. Because stories contain words not common in daily conversation, this is an excellent way to expand vocabulary.

The Common Core State Standards and Vocabulary

If you are in a state that has adopted the Common Core State Standards, it is the vocabulary of these standards that will be necessary for your students to learn. Therefore, teachers and parents should become familiar with these.

The list that follows sets out fifty words from the reading standards and the sample assessment questions provided in Appendix B of the Common Core. These are the nouns and verbs students must master so they become part of their automatic vocabulary:

Nouns	Verbs
alliteration	analyze
argument	articulate
analogies	cite
central idea	compare
conclusions	comprehend
connections	contrast
connotative	delineate
details	demonstrate
evidence	describe
figurative	determine
illustrations	develop
interaction	distinguish
metaphor	draw
mood	evaluate
point of view	explain
rhetoric	identify
simile	infer
stanza	integrate
structures	interpret
theme	introduce
tone	locate
	organize
	paraphrase
	refer
	retell
	suggest
	summarize
	support
	synthesize
	trace

It is not that we have neglected teaching these words. Rather, it is rather that often we have taught the concepts, but the words themselves are not cemented in children's brains. I had my students write descriptions on a regular basis. But in fact I never stopped and asked, "What does *describe* mean?" and then teach that word the way I taught other vocabulary words. When I ask a student to describe what he or she sees, some cannot do it because they have not stored the definition of *describe*. I probably gave them so many cues for the word when I asked them to describe (e.g., "Write what you see") that they relied on those other words.

Two other things will be occurring that may interfere with success on assessments. First, if the students are taking computerized tests, they must also be masters of the keyboard or they will be using precious working memory space and time on the clock to hunt and peck for keys. Second, they must be able to understand what the assessment is asking of them in order to answer the question.

The Common Core College and Career Readiness Anchor Standards for Language

For grades K–5, the following anchor standards state what students should know and be able to do relative to vocabulary:

1. Determine or clarify the meaning of unknown and multiple-meaning words and phrases by using context clues, analyzing meaningful word parts, and consulting general and specialized reference materials, as appropriate.

2. Demonstrate understanding of figurative language, word relationships, and nuances in word meanings.

3. Acquire and use accurately a range of general academic and domain-specific words and phrases sufficient for reading, writing, speaking, and listening at the college and career

readiness level; demonstrate independence in gathering vocabulary knowledge when encountering an unknown term important to comprehension or expression.

In the writing standards, vocabulary use is addressed in the standard, "Use precise language and domain-specific vocabulary to inform about or explain the topic."

I am addressing this standard as it relates directly to vocabulary expectations in our classrooms. Standard 4 asks that students recognize words in context and evaluate their impact. In this sense, they learn a number of words as they learn a single one. Part of the process of teaching vocabulary is teaching the synonyms for words. We must also teach the nuances that go with each word to help children understand more of the text in subsequent sentences or paragraphs that use that word. For example, a text might use the word *ignite*, which has *start* as one of its synonyms. What is the difference between those two words? If we replace *ignite*, which indicates fire or flames, as in the sentence, "His passion was ignited," and instead use the word *start*, have we given the proper meaning to the sentence? Later the text may say that his passion cooled, so understanding more about *ignite* and *flame* may help students get a better grasp of other information in the reading.

Choosing Our Words Carefully

We know that in order to build background knowledge and aid comprehension, children must increase their vocabularies. Knowledge of specific terms is a kind of background knowledge.

Not all words are created equally. To be more precise, with our limited time with students, we must choose vocabulary words to teach that are important. According to William Nagy, professor at Seattle Pacific University, and Richard Anderson, professor at the University of Illinois (1984), by the time students reach high school, they will have encountered in print 88,500 word families—groups of words that have common features or patterns.

Since there are too many words to teach at each grade level, we need a system for choosing which words to focus on. In 1985, Isabel Beck and Margaret McKeown, educators and scientists, suggested that every literate person has a vocabulary consisting of three tiers. Tier 1 consists of basic words that rarely require direct instruction and typically do not have multiple meanings. Sight words, nouns, verbs, adjectives, and early reading words occur at this level. Examples of tier 1 words are *book, girl, sad, clock, baby, dog,* and *orange.* About eight thousand word families in English are in this tier.

Tier 2 contains high-frequency words that occur across a variety of domains and play a large role in the vocabulary of mature language users. Examples of tier 2 words are *coincidence, masterpiece, absurd, industrious,* and *benevolent.* As a result, tier 2 words may have a large impact on the everyday functioning of language. Because of their lack of redundancy in oral language, these words present challenges to students who meet them primarily in print. Because of their important role in direct instruction, tier 2 words:

- Have multiple meanings
- Are used in a variety of subject areas
- Are important for reading comprehension
- Are characteristic of a mature language user
- Are descriptive words that add detail

The Common Core Standards are asking us to increase students' use of tier 2 words.

Tier 3 consists of words whose practical use and frequency are low. These words are domain specific and are used for brief periods of time when we are studying particular content. Medical, legal, biology, and mathematics terms are all examples of these words. These words are central to building knowledge and conceptual understanding within the various academic domains and should be integral to instruction of content. Although they are useful while covering specific topics, these are too specific to be included in tier 2, the most useful tier for vocabulary building.

Right now, we need to know how to choose words for our vocabulary lists. How do we do this? As you read the following paragraph, identify the tier 2 words that show usefulness and utility for mature readers and the words that are valuable across content areas:

> The stepsisters looked curiously at Cinderella as the glass slipper miraculously enveloped her foot in a perfect fit. However did this wretched girl procure such glamorous shoes? How were her ragged clothes transformed into a suitable gown that would have dazzled the prince and caused him to be mesmerized by some beauty found in her dreadfully dirty and ordinary face? Surely Cinderella is delusional if she believes she can keep such a man of grandeur interested in a scullery maid long enough to live happily ever after!

The words I chose as tier 2 words are sophisticated yet would be in general use by a middle school language learner with a useful vocabulary: *miraculously, enveloped, wretched, glamorous, transformed, mesmerized, dreadfully, delusional, and grandeur.* You may have included *dazzled* and *scullery.* Although *scullery* is a word that is useful to understand in the context of the paragraph, it is not a tier 2 word. Discussing with the students the meaning of the word is necessary, but the work of several engagements with the word to add it to long-term memory is probably not a good use of time. There is no clear-cut way to determine tier 2 words, and the words you chose from the paragraph about Cinderella may be different from those I have listed. Age and reading level of students should be considered in choosing which words are important to teach explicitly.

Some schools have made their own lists of vocabulary words for different grade levels, and individual teachers have determined what words they believe are important. Marzano and Pickering (2005) provide lists of words in the teacher's manual for *Building Academic Vocabulary*. They then provide a six-step process for teaching those words:

1. Provide examples or explanation.

2. Ask students to restate the explanation, description, or example in their own words. This is an important step in creating long-term memories. Make sure this "recoding" (Sprenger, 2005) accurately depicts the definition of the word. If it does not, discuss the appropriate explanation with the student before misinformation goes into his or her long-term memory.

3. Ask students to draw a picture or some graphic representation of the word. According to the work of poverty expert Ruby Payne (2009), if students cannot draw it, they really do not understand it.

4. Provide several engagements, such as writing the words in their notebooks, drawing them, and discussing them. Research suggests that writing is good for the brain and memory, so using notebooks or some other platform for writing is important.

5. Informally discuss those terms. For instance, in small groups, let students share when they have heard, used, or read the word. Again, rehearsal is important for reinforcing and strengthening the neural networks that have been set up for these words.

6. Play games with the words. Games are a brain-compatible strategy for reinforcing learning. Actively processing vocabulary words in multiple ways allows the brain to store information in multiple memory systems, thus making access to that information easier with multiple triggers or cues (Sprenger, 2010).

Activities

The activities that follow may be helpful in planning vocabulary activities for your students.

Vocabulary Word Maps

There are various ways of putting a vocabulary map together. Figure 7.1 shows two of my favorite models. The maps should allow room for a definition, synonyms, a sentence, and a picture. You may want your students to add an antonym as well. If you are wondering why a student is asked to write the word in color, it is because some learners remember color better than black text on white paper. Choosing their favorite color also personalizes the experience.

Frayer Model

This strategy was designed by Dorothy Frayer and her colleagues at the University of Wisconsin to assist students in deeply learning vocabulary words (Wormeli, 2004). Students are asked to write the vocabulary word, its definition, examples, and nonexamples. Figure 7.2 shows a model.

Write the word. _____

Write a definition of the word. _____

_____

Write a synonym. _____

Write an antonym. _____

Write the word here, in color. _____

_____

Use the word in a sentence that shows its meaning.

Draw a picture showing the meaning of the word.

Class Definition	My Definition

Vocabulary Word

The Word in a Sentence	My Picture

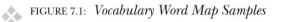

❖ FIGURE 7.1: *Vocabulary Word Map Samples*

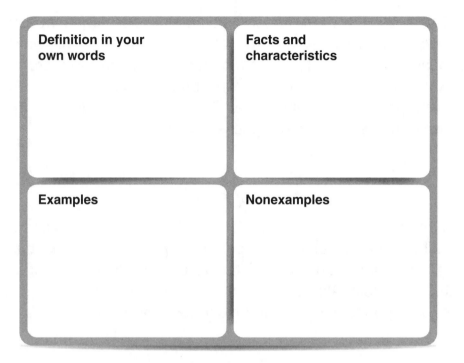

| Definition in your own words | Facts and characteristics |
| Examples | Nonexamples |

FIGURE 7.2: *Frayer Model*

Ready? Okay!

My students often wrote cheers to help them remember vocabulary words. It can be as simple as, "Give me a *C*! Give me an *L*! Give me an *A*! Give me an *S*! Give me another *S*! What does it spell? *Class*. What does it mean? STYLE! STYLE! STYLE!"

Leave it to your students. They will be creative and have fun, which will aid their memory of the word.

Freeze

Pass out vocabulary words on index cards to small groups of students. Tell them they are to huddle up and decide how best to portray their word and become statues in positions that define the word when you say, "Freeze!" For example, if the word is *ambush*, the group of students chosen to define the word may surround one student and freeze in a position that looks as though they are going to trap him or her. The other students must figure out what they are doing and guess the word.

Jeopardy

The Internet is a great source for finding slide presentations that are all set up to create a Jeopardy game with your vocabulary words and definitions. (I find the following site useful: http://jc -schools.net/tutorials/vocab/ppt-vocab.html.) You can divide the class into groups and have them compete for points.

Who Am I . . . or What Am I?

This is sometimes an icebreaker at parties. When you arrive at the party, someone puts the name of a famous person on your back. You walk around the room introducing yourself (your real name) and then ask yes or no questions of your new acquaintance to help you figure out which famous person you are.

In the classroom, you use vocabulary words instead. Write the words on index cards and tape one to the back of each student. Have them walk around and ask questions of their classmates until they figure out which word is on their back.

Say the "Secret" Word

This activity is similar to "Who Am I?" except students are open about the words they have. Write the vocabulary words on index cards and a simple definition on the back of the card. Tell the students that their mission is to teach their word to every student in the class, and it is also their mission to learn the other students' words. Have the students carry a vocabulary notebook or sheet of paper with them to write down the new words and the meanings.

Word Wall Bingo

If you have a word wall in your classroom with tier 2 or 3 words, word wall bingo is a fun way to interact with it. Have students make a large tic-tac-toe grid on a paper. Then they look at the word wall and fill in each space on the grid with a word. Randomly call out nine words from the wall. The first student who covers all nine spaces on the grid is the winner. You can then debrief the activity by discussing the definitions of the words.

Summary

Building vocabulary in all content areas is almost a full-time job. Take advantage of resources like Marzano and Carleton's *Vocabulary Games for the Classroom* (2010) and other sources mentioned in this chapter. Teach the vocabulary of the standards, and focus on building students' vocabulary or words in tiers 2 and 3.

CHAPTER 8

Comprehension

Reading It and Getting It

W<small>E HAVE LEARNED ABOUT THE BRAIN'S</small> language and reading pathways, including Wernicke's and Broca's areas, the language and reading areas. You will recall that Wernicke's area contains a mental lexicon of the words that we have learned. Some students have a lexicon filled with words from many different areas of learning and interests that they have. Six-year-old Jack can give you an enormous amount of information about dinosaurs and can also tell you a great deal about the streets in Chicago. If you ask me about the same content, I will have little to say. When Jack reads about these topics, he has the ability to "fill in the blanks." Interesting writers usually provide enough information for readers to follow yet often don't bore us with minutia.

Let's look at an example most of us can relate to: "My sister brought her small children to visit for the weekend. I had to catch up on my sleep on Monday."

Many of us will glean from the statements that I didn't sleep much because the children woke up early or didn't sleep through the night. Others might think that I took the kids to places of interest, and I was tired from the running around. If the writer continues with this story, it will probably reveal the reason for the lack of sleep. Readers with no experience with visiting young children may think the statements do not make much sense. They may then appear unrelated and not very interesting. When the brain can't make sense of something, it simply drops it.

See the differences in comprehension for the sentences that follow, which I recently read to four-year-old Emmie: "I am taking the new kitty to my house. Mr. Sprenger is angry." Emmie wanted to know why Mr. Sprenger is angry. When I asked her what she thought, she pondered for a moment and said, "Mr. Sprenger is sad to leave here." Emmie had separated the sentences and focused on what her background knowledge had been for only the second sentence.

When I changed those statements to "Mr. Sprenger is angry because I am taking the new kitty home with us," it all became clear to her: her eyes lit up and immediately wanted to know why my husband didn't like cute little kitties. Her background knowledge of kitties is from seeing them play, watching them on television, and reading about them in stories. If she had perhaps been read some nonfiction books about cats and their needs as well as their habits, she may have made the connection from the first two statements I made.

The point here is simple: we all derive meaning based on our own prior and background knowledge. As we look at comprehension in this chapter, keep in mind the importance of what students bring with them to the classroom. (And that was an example of such a dilemma. Are you thinking about book bags, pencils, and protractors? Or are you thinking about their experiences with text, vocabulary, and knowledge gained from other classrooms and from life?)

According to Dan Willingham, professor of psychology at the University of Virginia, "Kids who score well on reading tests are not really kids with good 'reading skills.' The kids who score well on reading tests are ones who know a lot about the world—they have a lot of prior knowledge about a wide range of things—and so that whatever they are asked to read about on the test, they likely know something about it" (Strauss, 2009).

Willingham makes a good point here. Let's pursue this idea, but with a twist.

When have you been a struggling reader? Author and teacher Doug Fisher has shared with his audiences a point at which he became a struggling reader (Fisher, Brozo, Frey, & Ivey, 2011). It was when he decided he wanted to know as much about the brain as possible. As a well-educated professional, Doug decided to take a class on the brain. We'll call it Neurology 101. The text that came with the course was indeed a book for someone with background knowledge or at least a large vocabulary about the brain's structures and functions. Doug basically said that the book was beyond his reading level. Just as a beginning reader like Jack has to stop to figure out his words, looking up words as an adult reads requires a great deal of patience as well as time. By the time both Doug and Jack get to the end of a relatively long and complicated sentence, they may be hopelessly lost. As an adult, Doug knows he must reread the sentence to get an understanding. Jack, however, may want to hurry to the next page, which may be easier to read, or he may just give up.

In order for Doug to get the information he wanted, he found a book that was easier to understand. It gave him much of the information that the harder text contained and allowed him to take a step-by-step approach to gaining knowledge of the brain. Jack may also need to find a book at a different level and work his way back up to the current text.

Teachers are incredibly talented at helping students learn comprehension strategies that assist them when they become stuck. We turn to some of these in the next section.

Modeling Comprehension

One of the most fundamental ways to begin to teach someone to read is to read aloud to him or her. I hope that throughout this book, I have made it clear that this responsibility lies with parents and other caregivers, language and literature teachers, and content-area teachers. When it comes to comprehending text, we must remember that the brain is hard-wired to mimic. This innate ability to imitate stems from mirror neurons.

By reading aloud and sharing how your mind thinks about what the writing is saying to you, you are modeling how any reader might approach text. This ability to think about one's own thinking is called metacognition. As expert readers, most of our reading strategies are automatic. If a sentence doesn't make sense, we often read it again to be certain we didn't miss anything. If that does not work, we may read previous sentences to see how it fits into the author's theme or ideas. When you share your process with your students, those neurons begin firing as connections are made.

When I present to teachers on the topic of wiring the brain for reading, I pose certain questions to let teachers of various content areas become aware of the importance of modeling comprehension of their particular text. I begin with the topic of literacy:

- Do you expect your students to be literate in the topics you present to them?

- Is there a specific vocabulary involved with your content area that is different from the vocabulary used in other content areas?

- Are there words that may be used in other areas that have different meanings from the ones used in your class?

- Whose job is it to teach these things to your students?

My point is simply that we are all teachers of reading. I know you have heard this before. I also suspect that many people who read this book are teachers of reading and literature. But if you have a self-contained classroom, you teach it all, and you are keenly aware that you model literacy for each subject that you teach.

Comprehension Strategies

There are many comprehension strategies that can be modeled. It is important that the students experience the strategy through the teacher's mind. In fact, if the teacher tries a strategy that does not work, the students will see that there are different ways to approach comprehending text.

Purpose

Most teachers of any content first want to establish why they have assigned a particular text. In other words, what is the purpose of having students read it? The often used KWL chart with three columns fits in well for establishing prior knowledge:

K	W	L
What I know	What I want to know	What I learned

I explain this chart fully later in the chapter, but for now, following the "K" and "W" parts in the first two columns will be helpful.

The teacher brings up the topic of study, perhaps the Civil War. Brainstorming together, the class fills in the "K" column with their prior knowledge of the war. Some of this will be correct and some may not. Time is taken to amend the misconceptions, and then the class proceeds to column 2: what I want to know. This column now establishes some purpose for the study.

Will knowing the purpose of doing a reading help the brain? Predictability is important for creating safety and security for the brain. Knowing what is going to happen and why allows the reticular activating system to function in its medium mode, firing at a stable, even rate that allows information to enter the brain and be transmitted to higher levels of thinking (Sousa & Tomlinson, 2010). This information also primes the brain for learning; that is, it alerts the brain to attend to certain information. For instance, if students read the table of contents of a book, some of the words and ideas they read will be stored in their brains. When they come to those words in the chapters, they may feel that the material is not brand new and therefore seems easier to integrate.

Visualizing

The ability to create the picture that the author is trying to paint for readers will help students throughout their lives. For instance, I often teach memory classes to baby boomers who are beginning to notice some slips in their memories. One of the strategies I teach is visualization. This is truly the easiest way to remember, yet many of us are not good at using this strategy. The brain dedicates much of its geography to visual memory.

When I introduced the Civil War to my eighth graders, I began with information that would form many pictures in their minds. Other senses were aroused as soon as the pictures were formed. I would begin by showing my students that I was indeed excited at the prospect of studying the Civil War with them. Emotions are contagious, and I want to model only the emotions that I want my students to also feel:

> Next week we will be beginning our unit on the Civil War! This is my favorite time in history to study. The women who owned the plantations wore the most beautiful gowns. But the slaves in the South endured some terrible living conditions. Many were abused by their owners, but didn't know what to do about it. Feelings about slavery were strong. And this war was the bloodiest war in history. I hope you can handle ALL THAT BLOOD! [The capital letters show the serious look in my eye and the tone of my voice.]

Then I was quiet, and so were they for a few minutes. I watched as their eyes looked up and toward the right and the left. They were creating pictures in their minds as they looked to the right and substantiating them with information I had shared and background knowledge as they looked up and to the left (Payne, 2009). They wanted to know more, and I had just the place for them to look: in their history books. The publisher had provided vivid pictures of soldiers in battle, slaves in hiding, and ladies and gentlemen dancing at balls.

Predicting

Do you ever wonder why we like to bet? "I bet you I know the answer to this one!" "I bet you can't hit the ball as far as I can!" The reason is that it's a great game for the brain because the brain likes to be right. Remember what I said earlier about the dopamine release that the prefrontal cortex likes? It turns out that whenever we make bets, our brains are waiting for the reward. That little extra push of dopamine and life feels good. Does it sound like a drug? It is for the brain, so why not feel good when it comes intrinsically?

Every time you ask a question and your students raise their hands, they are betting that they have the right answer. They are betting you will (or won't) call on them. They are taking a risk, but it's one the brain loves. If it's wrong and the dopamine is less than usual, the brain won't be happy. The good news is that the brain learns quickly, and it won't forget that one. It wants to be right the next time to get the dopamine treat.

Getting students excited about making predictions about their reading takes some effort. Remember that emotions are contagious, so if you model that excitement over making a prediction about what is going to happen next, it may spread around your classroom. The most important element is that predicting includes an educated guess: "Based on what we have read so far, this could happen."

You might start modeling prediction by asking students about their experiences:

Did you ever predict that something would happen and it did? What did you base your prediction on? Did you ever predict that something would happen and it didn't? What was missing from your information that made the prediction more of a guess? How is a prediction like a bet? Well, I'm betting that you all can make great predictions with just a little information. Let's begin by looking at just the cover of this book.

Active Questioning

Questioning is a type of predicting. When students ask their own questions, they are often wondering if their own prediction is correct. It follows that as we model predicting and its many questions, we tack on questioning, and questions lead to more questions.

When I taught middle school, questions were powerful writing prompts. After offering my students options for writing topics, I gave them time to choose a topic and write a one- or two-sentence synopsis of the story they were thinking of writing. They then formed small groups of three or four, and each student read his or her story idea to the small group. The listeners next wrote at least three questions they had about the story.

One of my students decided to write about a nasty incident that occurred while she and her family were traveling to visit her grandparents in Mississippi. Her story line went like this: "When my mom, dad, sister, brother, and I went to visit Grandma and Grandpa last summer we had to stay at a motel that we ended up calling 'The Roach Motel.'" That was all she wrote.

The students in her group all started talking at once. I had to remind them that they were to write their questions. They instantly began writing many more questions than required:

- Did you see roaches?

- Did you leave the motel?

- Where were the roaches?

- What was the real name of the motel?

- Had you ever seen a roach before?

- How many were there?

- Did the room have roach traps?

This ended up being a great approach to start my students in questioning. The students were directed to write their stories and answer as many questions as they could. They also were encouraged to ask their own questions, that is, to think about other information their classmates would want to know.

In order to get students to question what they are reading, the teacher must model this strategy. These are often called think-alouds, because you read to the students and periodically stop and tell them what question you have about what you have read thus far. For instance, you might be studying the Holocaust and decide to read an excerpt from *The Diary of Anne Frank* before you assign the book to the students. Here is how you might present the text and the questions that come to mind as you read:

"Our many Jewish friends and acquaintances are being taken away in droves."

Right now, my question is what the word *droves* means. I haven't often seen that word. From what I know about the Holocaust, 6 million Jewish people died. So I think *droves* means they were taking a lot of people away. Turn to your neighbor and see if either of you can come up with the word *drove* in another context. Where might you have heard or read that before?

"The Gestapo ... "

I remember reading the word *Gestapo* before, but what does it mean? I think that was what they called the German police.

" ... is treating them very roughly and transporting them in cattle cars to Westerbork ... "

I wonder exactly where this is. I think there is a map in this book that I should look at.

" ... the big camp in Drenthe to which they're sending all the Jews. If it's that bad in Holland, what must it be like in those faraway and uncivilized places where the Germans are sending them? We assume that most of them are being murdered. The English radio says they're being gassed."

Has she written about people being gassed before this passage? I wonder if I Google that if I will find out exactly what that is referring to. I can remember reading adventure stories in which soldiers put on gas masks before they threw containers inside rooms. The containers would break and fumes would come out. The people without the masks would gasp for air and cough. Do any of you remember reading or seeing scenes like that?

Often teachers use the question-answer relationship (QAR) strategy (Raphael, 1986) for questioning, which has four types of questions:

- *Right there* questions are easily answered by looking in the text. *Example: Who is the main character in the story?* These questions do not call for any critical or analytical thinking. These questions are fine to get the ball rolling as far as questioning is concerned, but we want students to reach into their own experiences and long-term memories to make connections with information.

- *Think and search* requires the student to think about the question and gather information from the text. *Example: How did the main character react to the others in the story?* These questions require a little thought as the student determines where to gather the information in order to answer the question.

- *Author and me* questions are answered not from the text but by drawing inferences from what the author has said. *Example: Do you think the author adequately solved the problem?* In order to answer this question, students must analyze what the author wrote and evaluate it using their own background knowledge and memories from other situations, either real or from another text.

• *On your own* questions also do not require the text: students use their own knowledge and opinion to answer the question. *Example: If you were lost, how would you feel, and what would you do?* Both thinking and emotion are required in this question. We know that the brain's emotional system and cognitive system are intertwined (Sprenger, 2010). This is an ideal time to encourage students to compare and contrast the situation in the reading with their own real or imagined situation.

Blooming Questions

I often joke with teachers about how we all probably have the levels of Bloom's taxonomy tattooed on our bodies. The fact is that using levels of questions really helps students see how much depth they can find in their reading. The original taxonomy has been around a long time, but the revised taxonomy (Anderson & Krathwohl, 2001) is what I use in my classrooms. With the new terminology, structure, and emphasis, I think it is more appealing to students, and I like the verbs.

Table 8.1 shows the levels of the revised taxonomy along with some examples. Students need to see how lower-level questions may be useful, but they also need to realize that generating and answering higher-level questions is good for their brain and their memory. The QAR system, as outlined earlier, makes good use of varying levels of Bloom.

The revised edition of *Classroom Instruction That Works* (Dean, Hubbell, Pitler, & Stone, 2012) emphasizes analytical questioning by the teacher. The authors suggest having students analyze presented information in an effort to find support, errors, and the perspective of the author or presenter. These all require higher

Table 8.1 The New Bloom's Taxonomy

Level of Thinking	Key Words and Ideas
Remember	Who or what is the text about? When did this take place?
Understand	What does the author want me to understand from reading this information?
Apply	How can I apply this information in other contexts?
Analyze	In what ways is this information similar to or different from what I have already read or what I already know?
Evaluate	In examining what the author has said, do I feel any differently about the topic or the underlying theme?
Create	What can I create that demonstrates my new knowledge?

levels of thinking, and teachers should model the construction of these types of questions so that students will be able to eventually construct their own.

For instance, if during an election year the students read the platform of one of the candidates, I might ask if there is any information that might be misleading or errors in reasoning. When the students have had the opportunity to determine the answers to these questions, they may be better able to ask questions of their own when presented with the other candidate's platform.

Making Text Connections

In their groundbreaking book *Strategies That Work*, Stephanie Harvey and Anne Goudvais (1999) encourage teachers to model three ways to help students make connections to what they read: text-to-self, text-to-text, and text-to-world. It is through these connections that readers can access their prior knowledge. These connections can start to be made as soon as students have read or have been read to.

Five-year-old Jack was listening to me read *Charlotte's Web*. At the point where Charlotte explained to Wilbur her purpose on spinning a web, I reminded Jack of a book on insects that we had previously read together. He immediately began to see that this work of fiction contained a great deal of fact, and soon his brain was making connections between the two texts. At another time, when I was attending a three-year-old's Halloween party, I helped with a learning center in which the children took large round crackers, spread them with cream cheese, and stuck pretzels around the outside to create a Halloween spider. Knowing that Emmie had listened to *Charlotte's Web,* I leaned in and asked her if her newly made spider reminded her of Charlotte. She smiled as she bit a large chunk of the tasty treat. Small experiences such as these make new strides toward making the text-to-self association.

Judith Viorst's *Alexander and the Terrible, Horrible, No Good, Very Bad Day* is a wonderful story to use for all ages to model text-to-self connections. Most of us can relate to Alexander's feelings about his life as everything goes wrong for him. Here, you can share an experience that you have had and then allow the children to share their own stories.

Sticky notes are excellent for text-to-text, text-to-self, and text-to-world connections. Students, in fact, love sticky notes! As they read, they can grab a sticky note and place it on the spot in the book where they find such connections. A simple TS (text-to-self), TT (text-to-text), or TW (text-to-world) can be printed on the note. During discussion or when writing about their reading, students can refer to the pages where the sticky notes are attached, reconnect with their ideas, and share them. This is great reinforcement for accessing prior knowledge and putting information into long-term memory. Reading the text and making the connection, writing on the sticky note and placing it where it belongs, and referring back to those notes provide the brain with three engagements with the material that boost those connections in the brain. Text-to-self, often an emotional connection, helps ensure that the memory will not be forgotten.

Table 8.2 Text Connections

Making a self-to-text connection	How did I feel when I read this text?
	What did it remind me of?
	Has anything happened to me that is similar to what is in this story?
	Do I know someone who has had similar experiences?
Making a text-to-text connection	Have I read anything similar to this?
	What stories or books have I read that relate to this topic or theme?
	What makes this story similar to others I have read?
Making a text-to-world connection	What is going on in the world today that is like this story or book?
	Have I heard about this topic or situation from other types of media, like television or radio?
	Have I seen information like this on the Internet or through any digital devices?
	Is my world similar to the world in the story?

I found that keeping a poster in my classroom with various questions for students to ask themselves as they look for connections in the text they were reading was quite helpful. Table 8.2 shows the questions. I also sent home a copy of these questions with the students to use as a guide while they read and did homework.

Before, During, and After Reading: What These Strategies Have to Do with the Brain

Every good teacher of reading knows that students need a reason to begin reading, one to continue reading and remember, and something to do after reading in order to process the material, reflect, and make connections that will form lasting memories. In their seminal study of memory and perspective, James Pichert and Richard Anderson (1977) sought to discover the importance of perspective in reading text. They wrote two selections, one entitled ''The House,'' a story of two boys who decide to play hooky from school and go to the home of one of the boys, and the other "The Island," essentially a story about flora and fauna on a particular island.

In separate studies, participants were put in three groups, and each group was asked to read a selection. One group was asked to read "The House" from the perspective of a potential home buyer, one group was asked to read it as though they were potential burglars, and the third group read it with no purpose in mind. After only two minutes for the reading portion, the participants were given a vocabulary test for twelve minutes and then were asked to write down what they remembered from the story. This free recall portion is important to our discussion of the brain and purpose.

A week later, the participants were again asked to write down what they remembered from the story. The study suggests strongly that perspective, that is, purpose, made a difference in not only what the people remembered but for how long. Purpose is crucial to the brain according to neuroscientific research. Therefore, whenever we ask our students to read, consider, think about, or work on materials, the more specific we are in what the purpose or target is, the more likely they are to focus on what's important and remember what they have read or gleaned from the information.

You may want to have your students read the following story, "Friends," with no prereading instructions and ask them to underline or highlight in pink the important details. Then ask them to read the story again, this time from the point of view of a psychologist, and circle or highlight in green the important details. Finally, ask them to read the story from the point of view of a burglar and box in or highlight in yellow the important details. On your whiteboard, chalkboard, or overhead, make a three-column composite list of what your students thought was important in each case. Lead a discussion in the difference of the lists when a particular purpose was established.

Friends

Tanya and Phyllis were best friends. They went everywhere together. Every Saturday, Tanya's mom dropped them off at the mall where all the kids in their class would hang out.

It was later than usual when the girls finally got to the mall: Tanya's mom was out of town, and Phyllis's mom dropped them off after her morning shift at work.

Phyllis ran ahead of Tanya to join their friends, hanging out in front of the jewelry store. Tanya took her time and gazed at the sparkling gems. She saw a diamond ring similar to her sister's engagement ring and was shocked when she saw the price tag: $10,000! "Look, you guys," Tanya squealed. "This ring is like Monica's. Do you think hers cost $10,000?" The rest of the kids oohed and aahed over the ring.

"Doesn't Monica have diamond earrings too?" Phyllis asked. Tanya nodded, now slightly embarrassed at her sister's expensive things.

One of the boys, Marc, said that he was tired of the mall and wanted to go somewhere else. They left the mall and walked across the highway toward their neighborhood.

"Why don't we go to your house, Tanya," Phyllis suggested. "Your mom is gone, and we'll have the whole place to ourselves." Tanya's mom and dad were divorced and her dad lived in another city. She saw him only one weekend a month.

Tanya shrugged. She didn't usually bring friends home, but she didn't want anyone to get mad at her because she didn't want them to come to her house. The truth was, Tanya wasn't as comfortable with this group as Phyllis was. She hadn't known them very long. She, her mom, and her sister had moved to the neighborhood after the divorce.

When they arrived at Tanya's house, she took the hidden key from under the fake "welcome" frog by the front door. The kids strolled into the house, and Tanya led them to the family room and put on some music. She moved some of her mom's fragile crystal vases and put them on the fireplace mantle. She didn't want to chance any breakage. They raided the refrigerator, where they found some soda and chips. One of the boys wanted to drink a beer, but Phyllis told him that was a bad idea. "Monica could come home anytime," she said.

Some of the kids wanted to see Tanya's room, so they all went upstairs for a tour. Tanya shared a room with Monica. The sisters had bunk beds to give them more space for their dressers, desks, and television. Some of the girls started trying on Monica's platform spiked heels and jewelry while the boys started playing video games.

Suddenly the bedroom door slammed open. Monica stood with her hands on her hips and started yelling: "Get these kids out of my room! I hate sharing a room with you. And take off my shoes and jewelry!"

Activities

The strategies that follow allow the brain to focus and make connections with the text or other reading material.

Before Reading

Anticipation Guides

These guides are one of my favorite strategies, and I use them in adult workshops as well as in classes with students.

The research behind this strategy is impressive. Reading anticipation guides before reading a selection helps activate long-term memories—in other words, it activates background knowledge (Head & Readence, 1992). The guides also generate interest because the brain feels challenged to predict possible outcomes of reading (Dufflemeyer & Baum, 1992). The reader's brain is giving opinions and making its best guesses as to the validity of certain statements about the reading. Anticipation guides can also be used after the reading for students to see what they have learned. They can change their answers or opinions at the end of the lesson or unit.

How to Create an Anticipation Guide

1. Identify the most important concepts you want students to understand from the reading.

2. According to the age of your students, create a guide with four to ten statements written in a way to stimulate conversation. Some of the statements should be correct and others false. The importance of debriefing and reviewing this guide cannot be understated. Some students think that whatever a teacher writes is factual. Therefore, let them know from the start that you may be trying to fool them, and their job is to discover which statements are not true. You do not want them to store misconceptions about the material.

3. Decide how you will present the information. Perhaps it will be on the board when students enter the classroom and you will also hand out copies for them to keep in their folders to refer to as they learn the new material.

4. Students need a way to state their responses. I often use "agree" and "disagree" columns on the paper. These columns appear before the statements and again after the statements. The headings read "Before Reading" and "After Reading." Figure 8.1 shows an example.

Anticipation guides are great for activating prior knowledge, piquing interest, and getting students involved in lively conversation when they know that their opinions count and wrong answers are discussable. Neurologist Judy Willis (2011) assures us that the brain desires the answers to its predictions, so most students are eager to read the material to discover whether they have predicted correctly. Whether they are right or wrong, the dopamine involvement in the brain encourages them to keep trying because being right provides such a good feeling.

Before Reading: Agree or Disagree	Memory	After Reading: Agree or Disagree
☐	Emotion affects our memories.	☐
☐	The brain can recall information from birth and throughout life.	☐
☐	Repetition is good for memory.	☐
☐	The amount of sleep you get affects your memory.	☐
☐	Nutrition does not affect memory.	☐
☐	Short-term memory lasts only seconds.	☐

FIGURE 8.1: *Sample Anticipation Guide.*

Give One, Get One

This brainstorming activity begins with the teacher sharing the next topic of study for the class. Students are asked to individually write a list of any words they can think of that are related to the topic. So if the next topic is the Civil War, students may list such words as *Robert E. Lee, Gettysburg, Lincoln*, and *Underground Railroad*. After an appropriate amount of time, students go around the room or, if you have put them in groups, around the group sharing a word on their list. If other students have the same word, they should put a check by it so no words are repeated. The play continues until all words are read. The person who has the "last word" is the winner.

This is also an effective review strategy. Students gather any notes or writings they have on the topic, create lists, and discuss what they have.

All of the Ks

The KWL chart, designed by Donna Ogle (1986), is used through-out the world as a before-reading strategy for teachers of students of all ages. These charts have been modified and changed through the years as teachers find that additional columns help their students in various content areas and at various grade levels.

The original KWL, which is still used, is a three-column chart, as I have already noted, with these headings, in order from left to middle to right column: (1) K, or the question "What do I know?" (2) W, or the question "What do I want to know?" and (3) L, or the question "What have I learned?" Column 1 is usually used as a brainstorming technique in which students share what they already know about the topic. Column 2 is used to discuss what they want to know or what the teacher wants them to know, or, usually, both. Then the pursuit of learning occurs through reading and various teaching strategies. Obviously this chart is then used during or after the learning to fill in the final column. Figure 8.2 provides a sample.

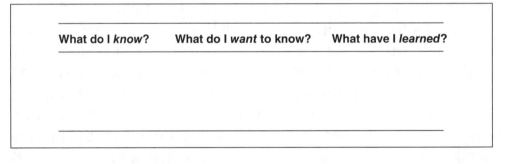

FIGURE 8.2: *KWL Chart.*

I began using a modified chart, the KWHLU, when I became more involved with differentiated instruction and relevance. The K, W, and L remained the same, but I chose to add the H for *"How am I going to learn this?"* I felt that students with different learning profiles should have some choice in their learning experience. Then I added the U to answer the question "How am I going to *use* this in my life?" So many students ask us why they need to know something, and this encourages them to find ways to use the information.

I am not the only educator who found tweaking the KWL chart helpful. Carr and Ogle (1987) changed the original chart to "KWL–Plus" when they added summarization to it. Wills (1995) made it KWHL and added *"How* do we know?" focusing on source information. Besides these, I have seen teachers use KNL where the N stands for "What do we *need* to know?" KTWL in which the T stands for "What do I *think* I know?" and KWLS with the S representing "What do I *still* want to know?"

Cloze Assessments

Cloze assessments, originally designed to test the readability of text, are used to see how students do with content and structure of text. They carefully choose a selection and substitute a line to write on for every fifth word in the paragraph. Students are then asked to read the selection and fill in the blanks using their understanding of syntax and context clues to write in a meaningful word. The goal is to find a student's instructional level.

Currently teachers also use cloze activities as preassessments of content knowledge. As a before-reading strategy, cloze activities allow students and teachers to see what students know about the content they are about to read.

See if you can fill in the blanks in the following cloze activity:

Find the strength and _____ in every student! Differentiated _____ enables teachers to plan _____ so they can meet the _____ of each and every _____ in today's highly diverse _____. Differentiated instructional strategies present the _____ techniques and processes that _____ can use to adjust _____ based on individual student's _____, skills, experience, preferences, and needs.

The missing words are, in order, uniqueness, instruction, purposefully, needs, student, classrooms, practical, teachers, learning, knowledge.

Choose a paragraph or passage from the text your students will be using for the next lesson or standard. The length of the selection will depend on the age of your students. Some cloze activities use paragraphs or passages of 250 words. Remove about every fifth word. Generally keep the first and last sentences intact. Retype the paragraph with lines to write on substituting for the missing words, hand it out to the students to fill in the blanks, and check their work. You will find in some cases that there will be synonymous words, leading to discussions about word meanings and how different words might change the meaning of the sentence.

Possible Sentences

Before assigning a reading, the teacher goes through the selection and picks out key words and phrases. She or he then gives a copy of the list to each student, and they are asked, individually or in pairs, to come up with sentences using these words or phrases. This strategy helps students become familiar with the words and the concepts they are about to study. Neuroscience research calls this "priming" the brain (Jensen, 2005). As students come across the words and phrases in their reading, their brains are more comfortable with the terms and concepts because they have used them before.

Think-Alouds and Read-Alouds

A read-aloud is the process of reading aloud to students with the purpose of modeling fluency and prosody. A think-aloud is the process of reading aloud and pausing to share with students what is going through your mind as you read, as was done earlier in this chapter with *The Diary of Anne Frank*. Read-alouds and think-alouds help students become interested in text. Using these strategies before the students begin reading gives them a jump-start on the material, including the type of reading they are going to encounter, and assists them in understanding some of the vocabulary (Fisher, Brozo, Frey, & Ivey, 2011). Although we discussed vocabulary in the previous chapter, it is appropriate to address again the importance of using whatever techniques are available to assist students in gaining an understanding of what they read by ensuring that they understand the vocabulary.

Pictures, Pictures, and More Pictures

We all know that a picture is worth a thousand words. No matter what the age of our students, presenting compelling pictures—photos, artwork, drawings—heightens their interest in what we are presenting.

You can use pictures to introduce a reading and help students make connections to a topic by finding pictures that are appropriate and interesting. Display them on your interactive whiteboard, screen, or even an overhead projector. Then draw your students into the topic and conversation by projecting a picture as they walk into the room.

One science teacher began a unit on gravity by showing a vivid picture of a boy on a skateboard doing an aerial while holding the board on his feet with his hands. The students were immediately talking about how cool the picture looked and what exactly the boy was doing. From there, the teacher led them into the conversation on gravity.

Word Sorts

Word sorts prime the brain for learning. Playing with words before reading them in context is a fun and informational way to introduce your students to new or unfamiliar words and will give you the opportunity to see how well students understand the words.

It is imperative for teachers to model the activity before asking students to do it on their own.

Creating a Simple Classroom Word Sort Activity

1. On a whiteboard or index cards, list ten to twenty vocabulary words from a specific reading selection.

2. Either provide students the categories to be used in the word sort (closed word sort) or let them choose their own (this is a more advanced, open word sort). For a closed sort, if you are teaching a short story, your categories might be: characters, setting, plot, and climax. The students would take the vocabulary list and assign each word to a category.

3. Create small groups of four to five students each, and have them work together on the activity, giving them ten to fifteen minutes to categorize the words.

4. Complete the activity by having each group present its word list for one category. This allows each group to present the reasoning behind their categorization and enables you to summarize the concepts and relationships of each category.

In the primary closed word sort sample in table 8.3, the headings (categories) were provided by the teacher and represent specific vowel sounds. The teacher then gave the students the list of words and said to put them under the word at the top of the column that has the same vowel sound.

Table 8.3 Closed Word Sort

hat	game	star
bat	race	hard
has	plate	car
mad	safe	park

Open sorts are a bit more challenging, and many students have fun thinking up unusual categories for their words. The teacher provides words for the students to sort according to their own categories: "Take each word and decide with your partner [or partners] which characteristics the words have that would put them in a category together. The words cannot all be in one category, and no word can be alone in a category." This type of sort can be done in any content area.

There are variations and enhancements to basic word sort activities as well—for example:

- Let students manipulate the words into more than one category. For example, both apples and pears fit into the categories "types of fruit" and "things that grow on trees."

- Ask students to explain the reasoning for their word classifications; often this can give you clues about where students need additional help and support in conceptualizing the relationships between words.

- Using pre-identified sentence structures (e.g., simple, compound), have your students form sentences using the words they have sorted to demonstrate they understand the correct use of the words. Perhaps they would write "Pears and apples both grow on trees."

Word Walls

Some reading strategies are useful for many of the pieces of the reading puzzle. Word Wall Bingo was included in chapter 7 on vocabulary as an important activity. Fisher et al. (2011) list word walls as a before-reading activity, but it is usually created before reading and used during reading and writing (Wagstaff, 1999). This strategy is not new to teachers of reading and content-area teachers for teaching vocabulary.

These words are written directly on the word wall or are made from poster paper or construction paper or whatever other material is handy. You may want to write each word on an index card and place it on the wall as each word is presented and arranged alphabetically. Students and teachers place or write words on the wall that are challenging, new, or just plain interesting to them. These may be words that the students will be encouraged to use in their writing as well as words they need to be familiar with for reading.

Building the Wall

1. Decide what words will be included on your wall. Will you need to keep space for extra words that may come along?

2. Choose a wall in your room that all students can easily see. If you are limited in open wall space, consider using a different type of space, such as the space above your whiteboard.

3. Select the material for your words. Will you use a piece of butcher paper? Construction paper? Something else? Whatever your medium, figure out how it will stay on the wall without hurting the surface. Paper that already has easily removable adhesive is expensive but simple to use.

4. Introduce your word wall to the students, making sure they understand the importance of contributing to it.

5. Add words slowly, keeping the brain in mind. Working memory holds only so much information. Plan on several engagements with words to get them into long-term memory if that is where they need to go. If the words you have on the wall are so specific to a theme or unit that students don't need to remember them for the long term, they can use the wall as a simple reference.

6. Be sure to make frequent use of the wall of words. Do quick-writes, an activity in which your students have a minute or two to write as much as they can about a topic, and other activities in which the students need to use a certain number of words from the wall.

Table 8.4 is an example of a word wall for the study of the American Revolution.

Table 8.4 *American Revolution Word Wall*

A	B	C	D	E
allegiance	blockade	colonists	Declaration	enlist
ally	Boston Tea	Continental	of Indepen-	
authority	Party		dence	
	boycott		democracy	
F	**G**	**H**	**I-J**	**K-L**
	grievance		independ-	legislature
			ence	liberty
				Loyalist
M-N-O	**P-Q**	**R**	**S**	**T**
massacre	pacifist	repeal		tariff
Minutemen	Parliament	revolution		tax
negotiate	Patriot			Thomas
	petition			Jefferson
	quarter			treason
U-V	**W**	**X-Y-Z**		
unalienable				
rights				
Valley Forge				

During Reading

Concept Maps, Mind Maps, and Other Thinking Maps

Graphic organizers come in all sizes and shapes. These visual representations help students know what to look for in their reading and help them remember. Today's students have spent a great deal of time with digital devices that offer them exciting visuals. Neuroscientists encourage the use of visuals in teaching (Medina, 2008; Small & Vorgan, 2008). Because these organizers are stored as pictures in the brain and students often remember visuals more easily than words, they give students a unique way of organizing their brains around the subject matter. Since the left hemisphere is language oriented and the right is oriented to the big picture, when words are placed in the graphical pictures, the brain is storing information in at least two places, which makes for easier access to the information for recall (Sprenger, 2005). Add to this the fact that there are digital tools that students can use to create these maps, and it's a winning combination.

Mind mapping was developed by Tony Buzan (2000) in England about thirty years ago, and Michael Gelb (1995) developed it further. I highly recommend these authors' books; however, many Internet sites offer information and examples, too. Do a search, or try http://www.mindmappingsite.com/.

In order for students to create their own maps, teachers must first model the procedure. Here are the steps I follow:

1. Turn a plain sheet of paper on its landscape side. You're also going to need colored pens, crayons, markers, or pencils.

2. In the center of the page, draw a cloud or any other shape. Write the topic or title in the center of the shape.

3. Draw anywhere from five to seven lines leading out from your central image or key word. On these lines, write one

word representing a subtopic. Use different colors for each word.

4. Add images, symbols, or icons for as many of the subtopics as you can.

For very young children, the map may be a series of circles and squares that contain pictures and very few words. For older students, there may be many more words, but pictures are still desirable for students whose memories rely more on visuals. Keep in mind that concept maps are used to show students how concepts relate to one another. Before designing a concept map, you must decide what concepts you want students to understand and be able to apply as a result of your lesson or unit. I have used my own concept or mind map to help organize my materials and my mind before I begin a lesson. Figures 8.3a and b show how a mind map and concept map compare.

Echo Reading

Sometimes students need to hear a text read and then mirror that reading for greater fluency. Students imitate the fluency and the intonation they hear from the teacher. This is done in small segments and continues until the end of the text. Young readers gain oral reading practice leading to the fluency discussed in chapter 6.

Jigsaw

This strategy, often used to cover material in an interesting and efficient manner, keeps students attentive and often motivated as they become experts in an area.

First, students are put in small groups, called the jigsaw group, with the number in each group dependent on the academic areas

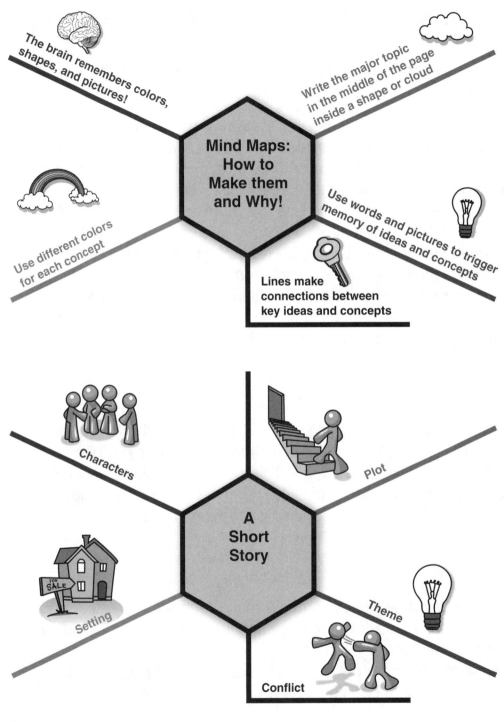

❖   FIGURE 8.3: *(a) Mind Map.*

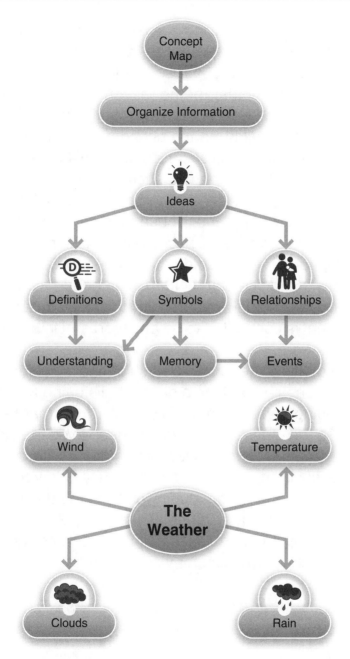

FIGURE 8.3: *(b) Concept Map. Most concept maps have boxes or circles for each concept that are connected by lines, with or without arrows. Concept maps help organize information for the student just as mind maps do. The technique you use with your students is entirely up to you and may depend on the content you are teaching.*

to be covered. For instance, if the group was learning about five reasons for the Civil War, there would be five students in each group, with one student in each group responsible for a reason. You can give each student a number for the reason. For instance, in each group there would be a student responsible for the first reason for the Civil War, which might be the economic differences between the North and the South. The second student in the group would be responsible for a different reason, such as slavery. The students from each group responsible for the first reason will form a new group, called the expert group. These experts will read about the topic, look over materials, and discuss what they should present to their jigsaw group. Then all students return to their original jigsaw group, each with a piece of the information needed to understand the Civil War. Each student expert helps to put the puzzle together.

Each student is compelled to be engaged and involved, first as an expert presenter and then as a good listener. Although each student may do his or her own research on the individual reasons, if the expert groups have done a good job, listening to the experts speak and being involved in the discussion may garner enough information so the other students do not need to do the extra work.

Like all other good cooperative learning groups, jigsaws provide a platform for social interaction, an opportunity for diverse learners to work together, and the opportunity for the students to save some time and learn from each other (Tomlinson, 2001). Jigsawing also provides movement for kinesthetic learners, conversation for auditory learners, and visuals for visual learners.

Read-Write-Pair-Share

Teachers often use think-pair-share, a cooperative discussion strategy developed by Frank Lyman (1981), to offer students the opportunity to reflect on learning and hear what classmates learned from the lesson. In read-write-pair-share, students practice oral language, writing, reading, and comprehension.

After they have read a selection, they are asked to write a quick response to a question or to write their impressions of the reading. They then pair up and share what they have written with their partner. The final sharing takes place as a large group discussion (Fisher et al., 2011).

Text Structures

Reading for information can be challenging for many students. All teachers should read a sample of the textbook to their students and point out how to read it and what to look for. Identifying text structures becomes second nature to good readers, but emerging readers and struggling readers need some pointers when it comes to identifying how the author has organized the material.

First, students need to become familiar with the different types of text structures that authors use. I use the metaphor of contractors building different types of physical structures to meet the purpose of the building. For instance, a home doesn't need a steeple, but a church probably does.

Each text structure communicates ideas in a different way. These are the most common structures used in textbooks:

- *Chronological order:* Events are given in a time sequence. Key words to look for in chronological text are *first, next, later, then,* and *finally*.

- *Compare and contrast:* Information in these texts identifies similarities and differences between at least two things. Key words to look for in compare-and-contrast text are *both, some, different from, similar to, like, most, otherwise, still, while,* and *although*.

ause and effect: This material shows how one thing leads to another. Key words to look for in cause and effect are *because, since, in order that, then, effects of, as a result, consequently,* and *so.*

- *Problem and solution:* In this structure, the author explains a problem and offers one or more solutions. Key words to look for in a problem-and-solution text are *difficulty, struggle, uncertainty, the problem is, possibility, hope, bright spot, future,* and *answer.*

- *Description or main idea and details:* This text structure is common but sometimes difficult for readers. Key words to look for are *for example, also, one reason, can be defined,* and *within.*

Text structures can be very important for readers to know when the topic is difficult or if they have little background knowledge on it. Using the text structure helps the reader identify what the author is trying to say.

Suggestions for Teaching Text Structure

- Plan time for teaching each text structure.

- Introduce the structure.

- Model how to read and understand that structure.

- If you are going to use a graphic organizer such as a Venn diagram (see figure 8.4) for compare-and-contrast, take time to show students how to fill it out.

- On the first day, read some text with the students and identify the text structure and key words.

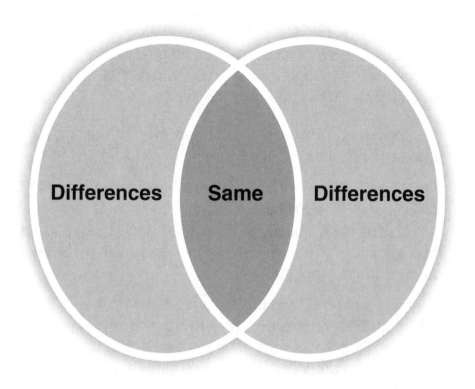

 FIGURE 8.4: *Venn Diagram.*

- On the next day, provide the students with text with the same structure and have them identify the key words and that structure for themselves.

- You may differentiate instruction by giving some students text in which key words are highlighted. Then they can match the words to the text structure.

- Keep reminding and modeling to students the fact that structures are a tool in finding meaning.

Reciprocal Teaching

⸍ technique involves four reading strategies, social interaction, ⸍nd cooperative learning (Palinscar & Brown, 1984). These are the four components of reciprocal teaching:

- *Summarizing* provides the opportunity to identify, paraphrase, and integrate important information in the text.

- *Questioning* encourages readers to identify the kind of information that is significant enough that it could provide the substance for a question. Then they pose this information in a question form and test themselves to see that they can answer their own question.

- *Clarifying* offers students the opportunity to make the text more understandable as they are reading. As a result, their attention is called to the many reasons that text is difficult to understand (another monitoring strategy). They can consult their peers to clarify vocabulary and assist them with concepts with which they have less background knowledge than other students. These students can also use reciprocal teaching to help make text-to-self, text-to-text, and text-to-world connections.

- *Predicting* requires readers to hypothesize about what the author might discuss next in the text, which provides a purpose for reading: to confirm or disapprove their hypotheses. This takes us back to the information from neuroscience about how the brain likes to predict and how the result of that prediction actually changes brain chemistry. An opportunity has been created for the students to link the new knowledge they will encounter in the text with the knowledge they already possess. Students can also use their knowledge of text structure to aid in the predictions.

At the heart of reciprocal teaching is dialogue. Teacher and students take turns leading the dialogue when students are deemed ready after appropriate modeling and preparation by the teacher. Good readers construct meaning from text as they monitor their reading to be certain they are understanding what they read.

Steps to Successful Reciprocal Teaching

1. Introduce the four strategies one by one. Be certain that your students understand and are able to apply the process of using each one. Summarizing is a good place to start because students may be familiar with this through retelling stories.

2. Model each of the strategies through read-alouds.

3. When the students are ready to lead, assign a short passage or story, and have students dialogue with you and the rest of the class as they use each strategy.

4. When students are clear about how the process works, assign text for them to read and work with other students to determine where in the reading to stop and have their teaching conversations.

After Reading

Question-Answer Strategy

The question-answer strategy (QAR) presented earlier in this chapter is more than a way of modeling for students; it also serves as a good after-reading strategy. When students have completed the reading, you can go through the four questioning types to give them the opportunity to think at various levels. Since "author and me" questions can often be answered without reading the text, I like to cover the first three types of questions to check for reading and understanding.

Exit Cards

Exit cards may be used as a preassessment or ongoing assessment but also at the end of a reading assignment. I sometimes call them "entrance cards" and use them at the beginning of class when students have had an outside reading assignment on a topic. The cards can help students synthesize information and reinforce memory. Besides assessing reading comprehension, exit cards can ask students how they feel about the reading and how difficult or easy the reading was. The cards should give you important information as to how well students comprehended the reading.

Exit cards can be devised in a 3–2–1 pattern:

"Describe three things you learned about _____ from the reading."

"Write two questions you have about the reading."

"Share one way you can connect the text to your personal life or to another reading you have previously read."

Some teachers use exit slips as "tickets out the door": students are not permitted to leave class until they have filled out their exit cards.

Steps to Using Exit Cards

1. From the reading you are going to assign, determine what information, such as facts or concepts, is important for students to know.

2. Create a question, a writing prompt, or a combination of questions using the 3–2–1 pattern. Explain that there are no right or wrong answers; you are simply gathering information as to how well the students understood the reading.

3. Give students slips of paper or index cards to address the questions or prompts on the exit card. Allow students three to five minutes to fill out their exit cards and return them to you as they leave the room.

Popcorn Review

The popcorn review, so named because students "pop up" with answers, is an after-reading strategy that allows students to have an interactive review of facts, procedures, and concepts. Explain to students that they will be held responsible by their classmates for what they've learned and will be given an opportunity to learn from each other. Students lead a discussion that reviews what they have read:

1. Ask for four or five students to volunteer for the popcorn review. (The first time I do this, I bring popcorn to class for the students.)

2. Have these students bring a chair or their desk to the front of the class.

3. Ask one of the volunteers to begin by stating a fact or idea from the text.

4. Ask another volunteer to "pop up" and add to the previous information or state a different idea.

5. The students may then pop up as desired as long as they are respectful of the other participants.

6. The audience should be holding the "poppers" account-able by looking up information or interrupting with pertinent information when it is appropriate to do so.

7. Allow this group a certain amount of time (five to ten minutes) and then ask for other volunteers.

8. If the review becomes too repetitive, make a statement to get the review headed in a different direction.

RAFT

This popular strategy promotes student writing about the text. RAFT is an acronym:

R   Role (of the writer)
A   Audience (who the writer is writing to)
F   Format (the kind of writing)
T   Topic (the content that is being written)

The purpose of RAFT is to give students an opportunity to think about the content creatively and reinforce their learning and memory by using a different point of view. Usually students are writing from their point of view with the teacher as their audience. Using RAFT will change that. For instance, students may walk into their literature class where they are studying mythology and see the following RAFT on the board:

Role   Zeus
Audience   Poseidon
Format   Text message
Topic   I am more powerful than you

Snowball

This cooperative learning strategy is helpful for reviewing information, summarizing and verbally expressing facts and information, and interacting with peers. Every student is accountable for not only learning material but also explaining it to another student.

Snowball Steps

1. After reading a selection, the class has a whole group discussion.

2. Students are asked to decide individually on an important concept or fact.

3. They write keys words related to that fact or concept on a piece of paper.

4. Students wad their papers into a "snowball."

5. When given the signal, they throw their snowballs toward students on the other side of the room.

6. Each student picks up a snowball that lands close by.

7. After opening and reading the snowball, each student finds another student, and they take turns discussing the information on each paper.

8. The teacher may ask the students to wad up their snowballs again and follow the same directions.

9. At the end of the strategy, the class reviews the points that were discussed.

Readers' Theater

Students read directly from scripts and are able to tell a story in an entertaining format without props, costumes, or sets. They do not memorize lines; rather, they interact with the text and express themselves with gesture and intonation (Worthy & Prater, 2002).

In addition to building fluency (see chapter 6), this activity improves student confidence in reading, and many students are enthusiastic and motivated to read and perform. Your students can create their own scripts from stories. These stories should have a lot of dialogue to make the scripting process easier. There are many Web sites with scripts already created, and that may be the easiest way for students to begin. (For tips on scripting, see Aaron Shepherd's Web site at http://www.aaronshep.com/rt/Tips1.html.)

Summary

Few things are as frustrating as struggling with reading. As Doug Fisher struggled at the beginning of this chapter, so have we all. Reading material that is appropriate makes reading more enjoyable. Having strategies to work on comprehension makes challenging reading a successful endeavor.

Graphic organizers are not worksheets. They are a vehicle for students to organize their thinking about what they are reading. Use them often, and use them wisely.

CHAPTER 9

Putting It All Together

T HE COMMON CORE STATE STANDARDS ASK THAT we go beyond explicit understanding of text to inferences and conceptual understandings. It has become imperative that our students learn to read complex texts, have the ability to compare themes and concepts, and communicate their understanding of both fiction and informational texts.

Our goal appears simple: we want every child to be able to read. Reading involves phonemic awareness, phonics, fluency, vocabulary, and comprehension. The brain must be prepared for the reading process through the construction of neural networks that will form lasting memories. Those memories include the process of reading, which must become automatic, and the concept of reading, understanding, inferring, summarizing, and demonstrating the ability to communicate to others. We cannot overlook the importance of encouraging creativity and reasoning as we all teach the literacy of our content areas and assist students in becoming the best learners they can be.

For Parents

Children who are to be successful academically most often begin their educations with an edge. That edge includes strong language abilities, a good vocabulary, the experience of having many books read aloud to them, access to print materials, and parents who love and support them.

Read to your child at every age. For young ones, crawling into your lap, being held gently, and listening to the excitement in your voice goes a long way toward raising a child eager to read and learn about the world. As they get older, share articles and books that you find relevant to you and your children. Support their reading. If you have a struggling reader, go back to an earlier chapter in this book and try some of the activities with him or her. Then move on to the next chapter, and then the next one, until you find an area that needs work. In a positive way, work with your child and your child's teacher. Create three-way communication among yourself, your child, and your child's teacher or teachers.

Wiring the brain for reading is not a natural process. It is necessary to make changes in the brain to develop the reading pathway. If rewiring is necessary—in other words, if your child missed out on a step in the process or has a reading problem—it is never too late to find it and fix it. It will take effort and support, and by working with your child's teacher and other educational professionals, it can be done.

For Teachers

It is always comforting to have students in your classroom who can read fluently and comprehend what they are reading because grade-level reading and beyond is an accomplishment that can lead to deep understanding. All teachers have a literacy to teach. The sciences, social sciences, mathematics, the arts, and music have their own vocabularies and their own languages. It behooves us all to teach our students to read our content by modeling how that is done.

Read aloud to your students from whatever materials they will be reading on their own. Show them how to read it, where to pause, what is important, and what they might skip. If they have the ability to read and understand your content, they will feel successful and be motivated to learn. Engagement in learning is key; reading and understanding foster that engagement.

Keep Learning About the Brain

Understanding how the brain learns and learns to read can help you and your children, whether your own children or your students. Creating environments at home and at school that make learning more desirable can lead to a less stressful experience. Our children don't always know what they need, and sometimes they have trouble organizing their time due to the number of digital messages they receive so frequently. Use technology as a tool to help children learn, and recognize when technology is taking up too much of their time.

The most important piece of the learning puzzle is the relationships in children's lives. Work on your relationship with every child and help them form strong social relationships that include face-to-face time.

I end this book with one of my favorite quotes, from Dr. Seuss in "I Can Read with My Eyes Shut!": "The more you read, the more things you will know. The more that you learn, the more places you'll go."

In my words: Read; know.

References

Adams, M., Foorman, B., Lundberg, V., & Beeler, T. (2004). *Phonemic awareness in young children*. Baltimore, MD: Paul Brookes.

Adams, M. J. (1990). *Beginning to read: Thinking and learning about print*. Cambridge, MA: MIT Press.

Ahmed, S., & Lombardino, L. (2000). Invented spelling: An assessment and intervention protocol for kindergarten children. *Communication Disorders Quarterly, 22*, 19–28

Alaimo, K., Olson, C. M., & Frongillo, E. A. (2002). Family food insufficiency, but not low family income, is positively associated with dysthymia and suicide symptoms in adolescents. *Journal of Nutrition, 132*, 719–725.

American Academy of Pediatrics. (2005). *Caring for your young baby and child*. New York, NY: Bantam.

Anderson, L. W., & Krathwohl, D. R. (Eds.). (2001). *A taxonomy for learning, teaching and assessing: A revision of Bloom's Taxonomy of educational outcomes: Complete edition*. New York, NY: Longman.

Arendal, L., & Mann, V. (2000). *Fast forward reading: Why it works*. Berkeley, CA: Scientific Learning.

Augustine, S. (2007). *The hungry brain*. Thousand Oaks, CA: Corwin Press.

Baddeley, A. D. (1999). *Essentials of human memory*. Hove, England: Psychology Press.

Bear, D. R., Invernizzi, M., Templeton, S., & Johnston, F. (2008). *Words their way: Word study for phonics, spelling, and vocabulary instruction* (4th ed.). Upper Saddle River, NJ: Prentice Hall.

Beck, I., & McKeown, M. (1985). Teaching vocabulary: Making the instruction fit the goal. *Educational Perspectives, 23*(1), 11–15.

Beers, K. (2003). *When kids can't read.* Portsmouth, NH: Heineman.

Berk, L. (2001). *Awakening children's minds.* New York, NY: Oxford University Press.

Blakeslee, S. (2000, April 30). *Sleep important to learning.* Englewood, CO: Colorado Reading Center. Retrieved from http://www.coloradoreading.com/Sleep%20Need.htm

Bodnar, M. (2011, February 23). Read and Ride: Newsroom programs come to D93. *Local News 8.com.* Retrieved from http://www.localnews8.com/news/26988834/detail.html

Bond, G. L., & Dykstra, R. (1967). The cooperative research programme in first grade instruction. *Reading Research Quarterly, 2,* 10–141.

Bourtchouladze, R. (2002). *Memories are made of this.* New York, NY: Columbia University Press.

Brand, M., & Brand, G. (2006). *Practical fluency: Classroom perspectives, grades K-6.* Portland, ME: Stenhouse.

Bronson, P., & Merryman, A. (2009). *Nurture shock: New thinking about children.* New York, NY: Hatchett Book Group.

Brookes, C. (2006, January). *Teaching literacy with the young brain in mind.* Presentation at the Learning Brain Expo, San Diego, CA.

Buzan, T. (2000). *Head first.* Glasgow, Scotland: Bath Press Colourbooks.

Cameron, A. (2012). Saskatoon method. Retrieved from http://sparkinglife.org/page/successful-school-fitness-models

Carr, E., & Ogle, D. (1987). K-W-L plus: A strategy for comprehension and summarization. *Journal of Reading, 30,* 626–631.

Christie, J., Enz, B., & Vukelich, C. (2007). *Teaching language and literacy: Preschool through the elementary grades* (3rd ed.). New York, NY: Allyn & Bacon.

Clark, C., with Burke, D. (2012). *Boys' Reading Commission: A review of existing research to underpin the commission.* London, England: National Literacy Trust.

Common Core State Standards Initiative. (2010). Common Core State Standards for English language arts and literacy in history/social studies, science and technical subjects. Retrieved from www.corestandards.org/ELA-literacy/RF/3.

Cowan, N. (2001). The magical number 4 in short-term memory: A reconsideration of mental storage capacity. *Behavioral and Brain Sciences, 24*(1), 87–114.

Dean, C. B., Hubbell, E. R., Pitler, H., & Stone, B. (2012). *Classroom instruction that works.* Arlington, VA: ASCD.

Dehaene, S. (2009). *Reading in the brain.* New York, NY: Viking.

Dement, W. (1999). *The promise of sleep.* New York, NY: Dell.

Diamond, M. (1997). *Magic trees of the mind.* New York, NY: Penguin.

Doidge, N. (2007). *The brain that changes itself.* New York, NY: Viking Penguin.

Dufflemeyer, F., & Baum, D. (1992). The extended anticipation guide revisited. *Journal of Reading, 35*(8), 654–656.

Elias, M., & Arnold, H. (Eds.). (2006). *The educator's guide to emotional intelligence and academic achievement: Social-emotional learning in the classroom.* Thousand Oaks, CA: Corwin Press.

Eliot, L. (2006). Infant brain. In S. Feinstein (Ed.), *The Praeger handbook of learning and the brain* (pp. 251–255). Westport, CT: Praeger.

Eliot, L. (2009). *Pink brain, blue brain.* Boston, MA: Houghton Mifflin Harcourt.

Fisher, D., Brozo, W., Frey, N., & Ivey, G. (2011). *Instructional routines to develop content literacy.* New York, NY: Pearson

Fox, M. (2001). *Reading magic.* San Diego, CA: Harcourt.

Gelb, M. (1995). *Mind mapping.* New York, NY: Simon & Schuster.

Giannetti, C., & Sagarese, M. (2001). *Cliques.* New York, NY: Random House.

Goldstein, M., Bornstein, M., Schwade, J., Baldwin, F., & Brandstadter, R. (2007). *Five-month-old infants have learned the value of babbling.* Poster presented at the biennial meeting of the Society for Research in Child Development, Boston, MA.

Griffith, L. W., & Rasinski, T. V. (2004). A focus on fluency: How one teacher incorporated fluency with her reading curriculum. *Reading Teacher, 58,* 126–137.

Gurian, M. (2007). *Nurture the nature.* San Francisco, CA: Jossey-Bass.

Gurian, M., Henley, P., & Trueman, T. (2001). *Boys and girls learn differently: A guide for teachers and parents.* San Francisco, CA: Jossey-Bass.

Hannaford, C. (2005). *Smart moves: Why learning is not all in your head* (2nd ed.). Salt Lake City, UT: Great River Books.

Hart, B., & Risley, T. (1995). *Meaningful differences in the everyday experiences of young American children.* Baltimore, MD: Paul Brookes.

Hart, B., & Risley, T. (2003). The early catastrophe: The 30 million word gap. *American Educator, 27,* 4–9.

Harvey, S., & Goudvais, A. (1999). *Strategies that work.* Markham, Ontario: Pembroke Publishers.

Head, M., & Readence, J. (1992). Anticipation guides: Using prediction to promote learning from text. In E. K. Dishner, T. W. Bean, J. E. Readence, & D. W. Moore (Eds.), *Reading in the content areas: Improving classroom instruction* (3rd ed., pp. 227–233). Dubuque, IA: Kendall/Hunt.

Healy, J. (2010). *Different learners: Identifying, preventing, and treating your child's learning problems.* New York, NY: Simon & Schuster.

Heschong Mahone Group. (1999, August 20). Daylighting in schools: An investigation into the relationship between daylighting and human performance. In *Pacific Gas and Electric Company Report, on Behalf of the California Board for Energy Efficiency Third Party Program.*

Hoeft, F. (2010, February 18). *Predicting children's reading skills using brain scans.* Presentation at the Learning and the Brain Conference, San Francisco, CA.

Iacoboni, M. (2009). *Mirroring people.* New York, NY: Farrar, Straus and Giroux.

James, S. (2008, May 7). Wild child speechless after tortured life. ABC News. Retrieved from http://abcnews.go.com /Health/story?id=4804490&page=4

Jensen, E. (2005). *Teaching with the brain in mind* (2nd ed.). Alexandria, VA: ASCD.

Jyoti, D., Frongillo, E., & Jones, S. (2005). Food insecurity affects school children's academic performance, weight gain, and social skills. *Journal of Nutrition, 135,* 2831–2839.

Kagan, J., & Herschkowitz, N. (2005). *A young mind in a growing brain.* Mahwah, NJ: Erlbaum.

Kaye, P. (1984). *Games for reading.* New York, NY: Pantheon.

Kuhl, P. (2007). Is speech learning grated by the social brain? *Developmental Science, 10*(1), 110–120.

Kuller, R., & Lindsten, C. (1992). Health and behavior of children in classrooms with and without windows. *Journal of Environmental Psychology, 12,* 305–317.

Kusche, C. A., & Greenberg, M. T. (2006). Emotional learning: An introduction for educators. In M. Elias & H. Arnold (Eds.), *The educator's guide to emotional intelligence and academic achievement* (pp. 15–34). Thousand Oaks, CA: Corwin Press.

Leitzell, K. (2008). The other brain cells. *Scientific American Mind, 19,* 7.

Lewkowicz, D., & Hansen-Tift, A. (2012). Infants deploy selective attention to the mouth of a talking face when learning speech. *Proceedings of National Academy of Sciences, 109,* 1431–1436.

Lindamood, P. (1995). Lindamood-Bell processes overview. In C. W. McIntyre and J. S. Pickering (Eds.), *Clinical studies of multisensory structured language education* (pp. 97–99). Salem, OR: International Multisensory Structured Language Education Council.

Lombardino, L., & Ahmed, S. (2000). The role of the speech-language pathologist in assessing and facilitating spelling skills. *Topics in Language Disorders, 22,* 19–28.

Lyman, F. (1981). *The responsive classroom discussion: The inclusion of all students. Mainstreaming Digest* (University of Maryland, College Park).

Marzano, R., & Carleton, L. (2010). *Vocabulary games for the classroom.* Centennnial, CO: Marzano Research Laboratory.

Marzano, R., & Pickering, D. (2005) *Building academic vocabulary teacher's manual.* Arlington, VA: ASCD.

Marzano, R. J., & Kendall, J. S. (1996). *A comprehensive guide to designing standards-based districts, schools, and classrooms.* Alexandria, VA: ASCD.

Maslow, A., & Lowery, R. (Ed.). (1998). *Toward a psychology of being* (3rd ed.). New York, NY: Wiley.

McBride-Chang, C. (1999). The ABC's of the ABC's: The development of letter-name and letter-sound knowledge. *Merrill-Palmer Quarterly, 45,* 285–308.

McEwen, B. (2002). *The end of stress as we know it.* Washington, DC: Joseph Henry Press.

Medina, J. (2008). *Brain rules.* Seattle, WA: Pear Press.

Miller, G. A. (1956). The magical number seven, plus or minus two: Some limits on our capacity for processing information. *Psychological Review, 63(2),* 81–97.

Moats, L., & Hall, S. (1998). *Straight talk about reading: How parents can make a difference during the early years.* New York, NY: Sopris.

Nagy, W., & Anderson, R. C. (1984). How many words are there in printed school English? *Reading Research Quarterly, 19,* 304–330.

National Governors Association Center for Best Practices, Council of Chief State School Officers. (2010). *Common Core State Standards.* Washington, DC: National Governors Association Center for Best Practices, Council of Chief State School Officers.

National Literacy Panel. (2008). *Developing early literacy: Report of the National Early Literacy Panel.* Washington, DC: National Institute for Literacy.

Ogle, D. (1986). K-W-L: A teaching model that develops active reading of expository text. *Reading Teacher, 39,* 564–570.

Oller, D. K. (2010). Vocal motoric foundations of spoken language: A commentary on Iverson's "Developing language in a developing body: The relationship between motor development and language development." *Journal of Child Language, 37,* 275–279.

Palinscar, A. S., & Brown, A. L. (1984). Reciprocal teaching of comprehension-fostering and comprehension-monitoring activities. *Cognition and Instruction, 2,* 117–175.

Payne, R. (2009). *A framework for understanding poverty.* Highlands, TX: Aha Process.

Pearson, P., & Gallagher, M. (1983). The instruction of reading comprehension. *Contemporary Educational Psychology, 8,* 317–344.

Pichert, J. W., & Anderson, R. C. (1977). Taking different perspectives on a story. *Journal of Educational Psychology 69,* 309–315.

Raphael, T. (1986). Teaching question-answer relationships, revisited. *The Reading Teacher, 39*(6), 516–522.

Rapp, D. (1997). *Is this your child's world? How schools and homes are making our children sick.* New York, NY: Bantam.

Rasinski, T., & Griffith, L. (2011). *Fluency through practice and performance.* Huntington Beach, CA: Shell Education.

Ratey, J. (2008). *Spark: The new revolutionary science of exercise and the brain.* New York, NY: Little, Brown.

Routman, R. (2003). *Reading essentials.* Portsmouth, NH: Heineman.

Shaywitz, B., Shaywitz, S., Blachman, B., Pugh, K., Fulbright, R., Skudlarski, P., et al. (2004). Development of left occipito-temporal systems for skilled reading in children after a phonologically-based intervention. *Biological Psychiatry, 55,* 926–933.

Shaywitz, S. (2003). *Overcoming dyslexia.* New York, NY: Knopf.

Sleeper, A. (2007). *Speech and language.* New York, NY: Chelsea House.

Small, G. (2002). *The memory bible.* New York, NY: Hyperion Press.

Small, G., & Vorgan, G. (2008). *iBrain: Surviving the technological alteration of the modern mind.* New York, NY: HarperCollins.

Sousa, D. (Ed.). (2010). *Mind, brain and education.* Bloomington, IN: Solution Tree.

Sousa, D., & Tomlinson, C. (2010). *Differentiation and the brain.* Bloomington, IN: Solution Tree.

Sprenger, M. (2005). *How to teach so students remember.* Arlington, VA: ASCD.

Sprenger, M. (2008). *The developing brain.* Thousand Oaks, CA: Corwin Press.

Sprenger, M. (2010). *Brain-based teaching in the digital age.* Arlington, VA: ASCD.

Springer, M. (2011, June 27). Turning point students rap to learn math. *Emporia Gazette.* Retrieved from http://www.emporiagazette.com/news/2011/jun/27/turning-point-students-rap-learn-math

Stamm, J. (2007). *Bright from the start.* New York, NY: Gotham Books.

Stanovich, K. E. (1998). Twenty-five years of research on the reading process: The grand synthesis and what it means for our field. In T. Shanahan & F. Rodriguez-Brown (Eds.), *Forty-Seventh Yearbook of the National Reading Conference* (pp. 44–58). Chicago, IL: National Reading Conference.

Stickgold, R., Whidbee, D., Schirmer, B., Patel, V., & Hobson, J. (2000). Visual discrimination task improvement: A multi-step process occurring during sleep. *Journal of Cognitive Neuroscience, 12*(2), 246–254.

Stoel-Gammon, C. (2001). Transcribing the speech of young children. *Topics in Language Disorders, 21*(4), 12–21.

Strauss, V. (2009, September 28). The answer sheet. *Washington Post.* Retrieved from http://voices.washingtonpost.com/answer-sheet/daniel-willingham/willingham-reading-is-not-a-sk.html

Tallal, P. (2007, March). *Better living through neuroscience.* Presentation at the annual conference of the Association for Supervision and Curriculum Development, Anaheim, CA.

Teicher, M. (2002, March). The neurobiology of child abuse maltreatment at an early age can have enduring negative effects on a child's brain development and function. STRESS sculpts the brain to exhibit various ANTISOCIAL, though adaptive, behaviors. *Scientific American,* 68–75.

Tomlinson, C. (2001). *Differentiating instruction in a mixed ability classroom.* Arlington, VA: ASCD.

Trelease, J. (2004). *The read aloud handbook.* New York, NY: Penguin Books.

Underwood, K. (2009, September 11). Actively reading: Goal of school program is to give children a way to burn off energy, build enthusiasm for reading. *Winston-Salem Journal.* Retrieved from http://www.kidsreadandride.com/Journal.html

Vaillancourt, T. (2004). Toward a bully-free community: The case of Hamilton, Ontario, Canada. *Teaching and Learning, 1*(3), 14–16.

Vygotsky, L. S. (1978). *Mind and society: The development of higher psychological processes.* Cambridge, MA: Harvard University Press.

Wagstaff, J. (1999). *Teaching reading and writing with word walls.* New York, NY: Scholastic.

Walker, M. P. (2009). Sleep-dependent memory integration. *Frontiers in Neuroscience, 3,* 418–419.

Wesson, K. (2005, July). *Scientific teaching: Merging brain science with the classroom.* Presentation at the Learning Brain Expo, Austin, TX.

Willis, J. (2008). *Teaching the brain to read: Strategies for improving fluency, vocabulary, and comprehension.* Arlington, VA: ASCD.

Willis, J. A. (2011). Want children to "pay attention"? Make their brains curious! Force-feeding won't work even on a hungry brain. *Psychology Today Online.* http://bit.ly/rtoI3a

Wills, C. (1995). Voice of inquiry: Possibilities and perspectives. *Childhood Education, 71,* 261–265.

Wolf, M. (2008). *Proust and the squid.* New York, NY: HarperCollins.

Wolfe, P., & Neville, P. (2004). *Building the reading brain.* Thousand Oaks, CA: Corwin Press.

Wolfe, P., & Neville, P. (2009). *Building the reading brain, second edition.* Thousand Oaks, CA: Corwin Press.

Wormeli, R. (2004). *Summarization in any subject.* Arlington, VA: ASCD.

Worthy, J., & Prater, K. (2002). "I thought about it all night": Readers theater for reading fluency and motivation. *Reading Teacher, 56,* 294–297.

Zimmerman, F., Dimitri, A., & Meltzoff, A. (2007). Associations between media viewing and language development in children under age 2 years. *Journal of Pediatrics, 15,* 364–368.

Index